Don't

Be

D1707407

Denied

God's

POWER

Revealing answers on how to get Jesus'
authority back into His Church for power
over sin, sickness, and the devastating
evil of these last days.

by Stan Riley

© 1993 by Stan Riley

Published by Joy Publishing
P.O. Box 827
San Juan Capistrano, CA 92675

ISBN #0-9395-13-79-X

Table of Contents

Letter From the Publisher

Every book has a story about how it came to be published. Some book's stories almost deserve a book by themselves. *Don't Be Denied God's Power* has such a story.

When this manuscript arrived in my office, it sat in a pile of other manuscripts for several months. I almost returned it unread. Then, for some unknown reason, I noticed it. I stuck it, along with other papers, into my briefcase to take with me on a cross country trip.

While on the plane, I reached in my briefcase and blindly pulled out something to read. I had grabbed *Don't Be Denied God's Power*. I started skimming it and soon was reading intently.

On my return I called the author. I told him that I felt I was to publish his book, but first, I needed to be sure that he could do what his book said. We arranged a visit.

I started testing him by taking him to a friend who suffered from a spirit of unforgiveness. After delivering her and then baptizing her in the Holy Spirit, her life changed on the spot. "I'm feeling like the heaviest load has been cast off my back," she said. It's been a year since then and there is no doubt about her deliverance.

Next I challenged Stan with a friend who had been diagnosed as having a brain tumor. We drove to her home. Stan and I prayed for her. At her next doctor's appointment, there was no evidence of a brain tumor!

The list goes on: back problems healed, eye sight restored and person after person baptized in the Holy Spirit.

I've been with Stan on several occasions this last year and wherever he goes, signs, wonders and miracles follow him. I know from first hand experience that the gifts of the Holy Spirit are real.

And that is the story behind this book. May it open your eyes to the gifts God has available for us.

Foreword

The purpose of this book is not to force a particular doctrine upon the reader, nor to contradict that of others, but rather to **encourage the Church as a whole** to open their eyes and ears: to consider the words of Jesus and grow in His reflection.

I make no claim to be the only or absolute authority on the subjects contained within this book. However, I can share with you what I have learned from my experiences over the past thirty-plus years in successful ministry.

The Christian Church as a whole, needs to take a fresh look at itself and begin to question its apparent complacency toward spiritual power.

This book will attempt to:

1) explain, define, and expose Satan's devices against the Church and its people

2) answer your questions by giving experiences of deliverances

3) show you how many ministries have been destroyed by Satan's intricately designed and planned traps. Satan will try any deception to ruin any one of God's servants and keep children of God from overcoming and obtaining eternal life.

Chapter One
Where Has My Church Been ?

Outside the gate of the temple sat a man who had become a permanent fixture over the years. Crippled from birth, he begged for his living, pitifully sitting there with his hand stretched upward. He hoped someone would drop a large coin into it, guaranteeing that he would be able to buy another day's food.

His legs were thin and weak; his faded, threadbare robe exposing the sharp bones at his knees and ankles. There were no muscles left in those legs after forty years of inactivity. They never would have supported his frail body even if he could stand on them.

Day after day, year after year people came and went. Each day those entering the city tossed coins at the poor beggar covered with dust from the streets where the throngs hurried to their jobs within the market place. "Alms, alms. Alms for the poor," he recited. "Kind sir, have you a gift for a lowly beggar?" His cries sometimes brought results, sometimes sneers. He had learned to play on the emotions of the women on their way to market, developing an inner knowledge of who might be touched by his circumstances. He was, in fact, resigned to living and dying by the city gate.

One afternoon as he sat in his favorite spot—the one where he had the morning sun to warm him and the afternoon shade—two men walked by, deep in conversation. Their faces indicated concern as they walked. "Better call out loudly so I will be heard," he thought. "Alms, alms. Sirs, men of compassion, have you a gift to share with a poor beggar?" They stopped abruptly. The dark, muscular man stared intently at him, and the invalid began to feel uncomfortable.

He turned to the second man, "You, sir, have you a token so a hungry man may eat one more day?" The men did not answer immediately, and the beggar, uncomfortable once again, turned his attention to others.

"Look at us," commanded the first man. Slowly the invalid looked up and met his gaze. The man continued speaking. "I have no money, but I will share with you what I DO have...in the Name of Jesus of Nazareth, walk!"

"Walk?" the invalid thought. "They cannot mean I must leave my favorite spot. I have been here for years. Surely they are mistaken into thinking that I am able to walk!" A glimmer of hope flickered across his face.

As if understanding his thoughts, the two men reached down and pulled him to his feet. Immediately those frail, lifeless legs acquired an unfamiliar strength. The astonished man found himself standing. "Praise be to God. Praise be to God!" he whispered as warm tears ran down his dust-covered face. As the coins tumbled down from his lap and bounced on the pebbles in the road, onlookers scurried to retrieve them before the man missed them. They needn't have worried. He was oblivious to everything except the fact that he was standing. No, he was walking. No, praise God, he was running and leaping! He was healed!

At another time, in another city, there was a slave girl possessed by a spirit of divination. She didn't know what it was called, but she knew she had the ability to foretell some events and had knowledge about certain things hidden from others. The girl had several "owners" who made handsome profits from her gift. They invited people to put her to the test to try to trick her, and if they could, they would receive a small prize. If, however, she discovered their hidden secrets, the participants paid heavily. It was lucrative game they played as they traveled from city to city.

During a stay in Philippi, the men's dreams of fortune crumbled. They allowed the slave girl to follow a group of people around that city. Her owners didn't understand her fascination with these people, but the girl spent every daylight hour following them. "These men are servants of the most high God!" she chanted. "They announce to you the way of salvation." Over and over, day after day, the slave girl sang these words as she danced along behind the small group.

One particularly hot, dry afternoon the group had stopped to pray. They formed a circle and bowed their heads. The slave girl heard, "Heavenly Father, attend to our prayer..." Again she began to circle the group, leaping and dancing as she went. She shouted, "These men are servants of the most high God." Over and over, louder and louder she heard her screams as though they were from someone else. Unable now to make herself stop, she was frightened to the point of wild terror, running as if driven by an unseen hand.

She briefly saw one man in the circle turn to her, and she thought he said something, but she couldn't hear him. Suddenly she dropped to the ground and lay motionless. The man who had spoken in her direction bent over her to help her up. He gently explained to her that he had merely said, "I charge you in the name of Jesus Christ to come out of her." He had spoken directly to the spirit of divination that had possessed her, and the spirit was now gone. It had left her immediately at the mention of the name of Jesus. She had been delivered!

Healing. Deliverance. Did those two incidents happen in the twentieth century? No, they happened during the time of the establishment of the New Testament Church. They are recorded for us in the Book of Acts, Chapters 3 and 16.

Can incidents similar to those happen today? Yes, they can, and in rare instances do. The question for believers today is, **"Should healings, deliverances and miracles be taking place today?"**

There is some disagreement on the answer. I have regularly seen healings, deliverances and miracles, and believe that they are the "signs and wonders" referred to in the New Testament seventeen times. Simply stated, I believe these events should be just as commonplace for the Christian in the twentieth century as they were in the New Testament Church!

Truly effective Christian living ministers to **every** area of life. The Apostles didn't see the beggar at the Temple Gate and just toss him a coin, making a mental note to pray for him. They weren't satisfied until he was healed. Jesus was their example. He had told them He was. He didn't see someone who was hungry and just say, "I will pray for you in the Temple." No! He **fed** them. He did not see sickness and announce, "I will keep you lifted up in prayer, brother." He **healed** him.

In Malachi 3:6, God said, *"I am the Lord, I change not."* Jesus operated in the realm of the miraculous in the past, He is doing so in the present, and He is interested in the miraculous in the future. Jesus is **still** our example, but you must readily admit that Christians are not as effective today as they were during the time of the early Church. **What happened?**

Jesus, and His vision, did not change over the centuries, but the **Church** did. The Church has lost the vision that **Jesus** gave it before He ascended into Heaven.

What is the vision? It is the same one He Himself came

to fulfill: He said;

> *"The Spirit of the Lord is upon me, because he hath appointed me to preach the gospel to the poor; he hath sent me to heal the broken hearted, to preach deliverance to the captives, and recovering of sight to the blind, to set at liberty them that are bruised; to preach the acceptable year of the Lord."*
>
> Luke 4:18-19

Jesus was reading that passage from the Book of Isaiah in the Temple to the holy men of His day. He told them that **He** had fulfilled that prophecy in their midst that day. In other words, He came to set the captives free and reach the world with the message of His salvation. Who were the captives? They were the people bound by spiritual chains. Some of them were the holy men to whom He was speaking. **Today there are Christians in bondage just as those holy men were.** Some are engulfed in chains so powerful that they cannot shake themselves loose.

The thought of **Christians** in bonds may go against all you have learned, but it is possible to be a Christian and be bound by things you wouldn't suspect to be classified as bondages. Such things as *fear, anxiety (i.e., stress), frustration, failure, antagonism, and jealousy* are all bondages. If you are bound by FEAR you know all too well that fear can torment you, paralyze you, and render you completely ineffective for God. Take heart though, because Jesus really DID come to set the captives free, and through Him you can be delivered from fear of **anything**.

As Christians, we tend to believe that only the unsaved are susceptible to these bondages; and consequently, when we think of ministering in deliverance, we automatically go to the unsaved. **I now know, however, through thirty years of experience as a pastor and through a fresh look at the Word of**

**God, that these problems are not solely the property of the
unsaved.**   This is a crucial point and one that I will be
repeating.

The lame man and the girl with the spirit of divination at
the beginning of this chapter were examples of the unsaved in
bondage. As we explore this subject further, you will see that
Christians can also be bound by emissaries from the pit of Hell.
Whether you are dealing with Christians or the unsaved world,
Jesus can set anyone free, and He uses **us** as His instruments
to BRING that deliverance. When Jesus told the men in the
Temple that He came to bring "sight to the blind", He was
referring both to physical vision and spiritual vision. SEEING
the bondages is the first step in ridding the Church of them,
and **then** we can bring deliverance to those who so desperately
need it.

Recent teaching has defined **abundant life** as possessing
big houses, big cars, and big, BIG churches. Unfortunately,
some churches are large only because of successful building
projects and programs aimed at drawing large crowds. Which
ones are large because they are exhibiting **the abundant life of
deliverance** that Jesus promised? Remember Jesus' vision for
the Church was for them to be **free** of sin, sickness, disease,
demons, etc.

> *"heal the sick, cleanse the lepers, raise the dead, and cast
> out demons"*
>
> Matthew 10:1-8

> *"all power has been given unto Me in heaven and earth,
> so therefore* (you can)[1] *GO, and teach all nations,
> baptizing them in the name of the Father, and of the Son,
> and of the Holy Ghost, doing **all** things* (not just SOME

---

[1] Author's comment added to Scripture verse

of the things) *I have already commanded you."*

Matthew 28:18,19

In other words, He was interested in ALL the areas where we need help, the physical and the spiritual.

As Jesus went about ministering to the TOTAL man, His ministry was approved of God. **How?** In Acts 2:22 it says that,

"Jesus of Nazareth, a man approved of God among you by miracles and wonders and signs,[2] which God did by Him in the midst of you."

How does God show approval of a ministry? Mark 16:20 says that God approves by seeing to it that **miracles, signs and wonders** follow those who believe AND are walking in the pattern Jesus set. Listen,

"And they went forth, and preached everywhere, the Lord working with them, and CONFIRMING THE WORD WITH SIGNS AND WONDERS."

Paul said that he, "through mighty signs and wonders, by the power of the Spirit of God... had **fully** preached the gospel of Christ"(Romans 15:19). Those evidences of approval went everywhere with him and confirmed the words which he was preaching. No wonder people believed the good news!

Our God is a **sign, wonder and miracle God**, and He is interested in putting His approval on "our" ministries by these evidences of His power. We do not "use" Him, but He uses us, and clearly demonstrates His approval as He did from Genesis through Revelation with all true believers. As we are used of God, He is **forming us** into the people He wants us to

---

[2] Author's emphasis

become—the image of Jesus—looking like Him, acting like Him, talking like Him.

Jesus will someday return to the Earth and claim the Church as **His bride,** and we are told that a Marriage Supper will be held in celebration (Matthew 22, and Revelation 21). These are events that WILL take place at some God-ordained time in the future and are not simply nice things to think about and dismiss.

If you and I are going to become the Bride of Christ, it appears that we are going to have to do some **serious** preparation. Even earthly brides spend months preparing for their weddings, and their approaching wedding dates make them plan even more earnestly. How much **more so** should the bride of Jesus plan and prepare!

Jesus will come back for a PERFECT Church, and you and I are that Church. We are the only buildings Jesus dwells in. We are not perfect yet, but as we walk **in the vision that Jesus gave us,** we are being perfected on a daily basis. EXPECT to see Jesus' vision fulfilled in your life as a Believer. Look at it often; keep it constantly in your frontal lobe, pondering it consciously, constantly working at believing it. Jesus indicated that as you minister, you can **expect** to see signs of God's approval. He said,

> *"Truly, TRULY, I say unto you, he that believes on Me, the works that I do shall he do ALSO...and GREATER works than these shall he do because I go unto the Father."*
>
> Matthew 14:12

He showed us what the Church should be, and His death made it possible for the Church to become as He was: **sinless, filled with and empowered by the Spirit, and going about the business of setting people free.**

The disciples caught that vision and entire cities were known to rejoice as they ministered with God's obvious approval. **Peter** (Acts 9:34-35; 40-42), **John** (Acts 3:7), **Stephen** (Acts 6:8), **Philip** (Acts 8:6-8; 13), **Ananias** (Acts 9:17,18), **Paul, Barnabas** (Acts 14:3 and Romans 15:19), and **many others** (2:43, 5:12) performed HEALINGS of sickness and diseases, DELIVERANCE of the insane, and RAISING of the dead, **again and again!**

Can WE operate in this area **again**? *Yes, we can.* This was HIS vision of us. The WORD convicts us that we are NOT yet doing what it says we *can do.* The works that He did, we shall do! HE is the one who said so. It takes commitment and working on developing our faith and authority in these areas. But anyone can do it, for with God anything is possible. That's what this book is all about for you.

Dear Church, you should not be content until you see God moving through you supernaturally! The Word says that Elijah worked many miracles, including shutting up the heavens for three years so there was NO rain. God said that YOU and I, Church, **are just like Elijah.** He had plenty of human faults that he needed to confess, just like us, but God worked through him anyway.

"Elijah was a man subject to like passions as we are, and he prayed earnestly that it might not rain: and it rained not on the earth by the space of three years and six months, and he prayed again and the heaven gave rain, and the earth brought forth her fruit."

James 5:17

Do you lack the faith to believe that God wants to work through **YOU like this**? Jesus said that even if YOUR faith is as small as a mustard seed, *"you shall say unto this mountain, 'Remove from here to another place,' and it shall move; and nothing shall be impossible to you."* (Matthew 17:20).

It is hard to believe that God still works miracles because the Church hasn't yet been encouraged **enough** to operate in the realm of believing God for the miraculous. But I am here to say that He has worked wonders through me for years. These wonders started when I caught HIS vision. He can do even more through YOU! How? By changing our **thinking**. The renewing of our minds needs to happen (Romans 12:2) until we have the mind of Christ (I Corinthians 2:16), that is, *Christ's vision!*

Seeing the church as vital, alive and a threat to the enemy (who wants it weak!), may appear to be a dream. The Book of Revelation indicates, however, that the last-days-**Church** (that's us, right NOW) **will be the powerfully effective weapon** against Satan that it was meant to be: "OVERCOMERS"(2:7, 2:11) and, *"them that had gotten victory over the beast and over his mark"*(15:2).

The **truly, believing-Church** will awaken from its lethargy and begin to speak the Word of God into seemingly hopeless situations. When THAT happens, the signs and wonders will be manifested as promised. Christians **speaking the Word** can expect to see the POWER following. *This is the norm. This is Biblical*!

If you are not being taught this message at your church, you may not be seeing the miraculous. But **you** can be the pioneer in your church to change this with **this** promise. The Book of Joel prophecies about the end-time-Church saying,

> *"And it shall come to pass afterward that I will pour out My Spirit upon ALL flesh."*
>
> Joel 2:28

This means you, and me, and your pastor and my fellow pastors. He will do these things now, and He **expects us to be ready to have those signs and wonders following us as we**

minister. He expects His own prophecies about us to come true!

To be ready, you need to be aware of the enemy and his tactics of deception against the unsaved AND **SAVED** world. Satan has cleverly and effectively stripped the Church of most of its weapons. An army without weapons is a defeated army. The church needs to see this, and to pick up its dropped weapons provided by God, and be **willing to use them once more! Don't be denied the power.**

Some churches **have** begun to do this. Most have not. The next chapter takes a look at churches and their historical progress so far. Come with me first, on this historical journey of His church, and then be a part of His own prophecies for "those who believe."

Chapter Two
Recent Church History

Pentecostals

The original Pentecostal Movement of the early 1900's was valid in at least one key area (regardless of its excesses, zeal and stigmas). This was when the clergy began to teach the church in areas that had been overlooked for many, many years. These early Pentecostal teachers promoted the miracle working **power of the Holy Spirit.**

Other teachers, like Smith Wigglesworth, Leonard Ravenhill, and Watchmen Nee were raised up by God to continue showing this Biblical POWER given to those pioneer Pentecostals that not only saved people, but also healed the sick and cast out demons. These men did not stop with just teaching alone, but **they showed the same power and revelation known to the Apostles and the early disciples** shown to us in the Book of Acts.

Pentecost was an outflowing of the power of God through the person of the Holy Spirit. However, this outpouring deteriorated into something to be "baptized into," instead of becoming a mighty force that would enable men to fully preach the Gospel with signs, wonders and miracles.

Paul listed the powerful **gifts** of the Holy Spirit in his letter to the Corinthian church,

"Now there are diversities of gifts, but the same Spirit. For to one is given by the Spirit the word of wisdom; to another the word of knowledge by the same Spirit; to another faith by the same Spirit: to another the gifts of

healing by the same Spirit; to another the working of miracles; to another prophecy; to another discerning of spirits; to another different kinds of tongues; to another the interpretation of tongues; But all these worketh that one and the selfsame Spirit dividing unto every man severally as He will."

I Corinthians 12:4, 8-11

Unfortunately, the Pentecostals were human, and slowly the **Gifts** of the Holy Spirit, which were sovereignly given, were replaced with unsatisfactory religious substitutes. The gift of knowledge was replaced by human experience. The gift of interpretation became rules and traditions. The gift of faith became human emotions. The gift of discerning changed into suspicion and witch-hunting. The gift of prophecy became intellectual preaching.

And so, in most of the church-world, **the mighty force that would enable men to fully preach the Gospel with powerful signs, wonders and miracles** became a mere "religious experience."

But for those who stayed hungry for a more personal relationship with the Holy Spirit, and who studied the Word, this movement brought them into a deeper walk with the Lord. It has also reached those who, for whatever reasons, had decided that Pentecostal teaching was not for them. It has now gone beyond denominational boundaries, even penetrating the so-called liberal and mainline groups.

Unfortunately, we still have separations into Neo-Pentecostals, Classic Pentecostals and Catholic Pentecostals. **These are man's divisions** that are not a part of the perfect church that Jesus will be watching for upon His return.

A. A. Allen, a great evangelist of the 1950's, brought back

to the church the teaching of the **true form of praise and worship he found in the Bible.** Old traditions had lulled people into just singing psalms without worshiping Jesus, the true focal point of true worship. Allen taught that through music and singing, Christians could experience a joy lost by the church. As a result, **Christians once again joyously praised as David taught** in Psalms 149 and 150,

> *"Let the children of Zion be JOYFUL in their King. Let them praise His name in the dance, let them sing praises to Him with the timbrel and harp. Praise Him with the sound of the trumpet. Praise Him with stringed instruments, upon the high sounding cymbal."*

That kind of joyful, loud praise produced the kind of faith which opened people up to receive more from God, in the form of **miracles and healing.**[3] People were set free from sin, insanity and diseases during Allen's worship services. Other leaders followed his example and found the same miraculous results. **This** Pentecostalism began to revitalize an otherwise slumbering Church, just as the one-hundred and twenty disciples in the upper room on the *Day of Pentecost in Jerusalem* came out so filled with the Holy Spirit, that their **joy, praises to God, and miraculous languages** made the onlookers think they were drunk! (Acts 2).

Some Pentecostals, in their desire to be accepted by the mainstream denominations and wanting to be accepted "back into the community," **allowed the Gifts to wane.** Compromising their uniqueness in God, they got bogged down in doctrinal arguing, and did not keep up the wonderful flow of the Spirit with which it had begun.

---

[3] Praise helps to transcend doubt, both in the congregation and in the leader. Doubt is an emotion, as is joyful praise. One cancels out the other. Praise also produces expectancy so that healing can enter.

Charismatics

Whether or not you approve of the next move of God, labeled the Charismatic Move, you need to recognize that it was a move **originated** in the Early Church. The Church did not now want to be labeled as "Pentecostal" (because of the emotional excesses that they had heard about) and so they began calling themselves by this different name as **God re-birthed the Gifts ministries** all over the world again, for God will not leave Himself without a witness of His power.

"Charisma," is a Greek word, interpreted as "gift" in I Corinthians 12:1. It means "gratuity," "deliverance," (as from danger), and specifically means "spiritual endowment or miraculous faculty."

The world may interpret "charisma" as some especially persuasive charm, but that is incorrect. A person does not "have" charisma; he "is" charismatic. One **is charismatic if he or she is endowed by God with the spiritual Gifts** listed by Paul. These Gifts, by their amazing, miraculous nature of the wonder of God's power and love, draw emotional reactions from us.

The fact that this movement of God **seemed** to disappear for a number of centuries does not mean that somewhere a remnant of believers was not operating in this realm of the Spirit-led life. It certainly **was** happening behind the scenes, as we learned later from books written by missionaries and other believers all over the world during that time.

It may make you uncomfortable to acknowledge Charismatics because you (like me) may have had an unpleasant experience at some time in your Christian life connected with their kind of enthusiasm (as I have). However, as the world is urged not to judge Jesus by all Christians, I would urge you not to judge this move **of God** by all Charismatics or by a situation you have found offensive. **God**

can show you anything you want to know about Himself, no matter what others do around you.

There are Charismatic Catholics, Charismatic Lutherans, Charismatic Baptists, etc. **They have tried to ADD the Charismatic experience to their worship, without letting go of religious dogma, and this has caused much confusion.** This addition may make better Catholics, Baptists, etc., but it does not necessarily make better Christians of them. Most successful Charismatics had to pull away from denominationalism and find brothers and sisters to grow with who were also hungry for that Biblical, Godly power.

The persecution from denominational churches against those in their midst who were seeking to be used by God in those miraculous Charismatic Gifts all too often sent those believers looking for fellow charismatics. Sadly, today also, that same persecution still causes hungry believers to leave beloved churches and begin attending another one where the **entire Word is taught that includes Jesus' total, POWER-filled vision for His church** (see previous chapter). A few are Biblically sound and strong enough to stay and help others see Jesus' vision.

I believe that historically most of those original Charismatic Christians stopped short of what God planned for that Charismatic Move. God's intention was for them to begin again to *walk more powerfully* in the revelation of the **full** knowledge of His vision, *not just feel it*. Charisma may be the **beginning** of what is available, but there is so much more for the Church.

Problems arose when Christians believed that being Charismatic meant being filled with the Holy Spirit in order to just "have a prayer language," and nothing more. Getting this ability to pray is a very important part, but a long way from the FULLNESS of the **gifted** life. True Charismatics are prepared to study His gifts (below) and then to be willing to walk in the fullness of the Spirit twenty-four hours a day.

Walking in Spirit-fullness can be done because God Himself has given us **decision-making power.** You **decide** to WORK at **consistently** increasing your *faith in His promises* and seeing those signs and wonders which we now know about. This will allow God to keep them in His Church.

God is still trying to find those who understand this and are willing to be used in *all the gifts*. "The eyes of the Lord look to and fro upon the whole earth, to show Himself strong (**power**ful) in the behalf of them whose heart is perfect toward Him" (II Chronicles 15:9).

So let's look closely at all the Gifts.

Word of Wisdom
I Corinthians 12:8

This is the first **gift** mentioned. It refers to God's wisdom, supernaturally given into a given situation. Man's wisdom does not enter into this gift, even if he is a Bible scholar or theologian.

"The foolishness of God is wiser than man."

I Corinthians 1:25

So this Word of Wisdom gift is not learned, but instead, it is appropriated, as are all the Gifts. "Appropriated" means seeing them and USING them as your **own.** The Gifts ARE yours.

Here are just two of the many examples of this gift in Scripture. First, King Solomon dealt with two women claiming to be the mother of the same child, after one had accidentally smothered her own to death. How would you have known which was the real mother? King Solomon's solution was to divide the child in half, knowing that the real mother would say to give the child to the other woman just to keep it alive (I Kings 3:16-28).

The other example took place when the Jewish leaders tried to trap Jesus with the issue of taxes which Rome demanded and the Jews despised. He called for a coin and asked them whose picture was on it. Then He told them to give unto Caesar that which was Caesar's and to God what was God's (Matthew 22:15-22). The Word of Wisdom solved a sticky situation and astonished his accusers. It was not just an intellectual answer. It was from the Spirit.

Word of Knowledge
I Corinthians 12:8

When Jesus was told that Lazarus was dead, he already had knowledge of that fact. He knew it by a Word of Knowledge from the Holy Spirit, and by that same GIFT He said He would raise Lazarus from the dead.

"Our friend Lazarus sleepeth; but I go, that I may awake him out of sleep."
John 11:11

This gift refers to KNOWING something in advance without having any natural way of learning it. Another example of the Word of Knowledge happened when Jesus told His disciples they could go out to find a donkey and its colt in a definite manner.

"Go into the village over there, and right away you will find a donkey tied, and a colt with her: loose them and bring them to me."
Matthew 21:2,3

And they found them, and brought them, just as He had said.

Gift of Faith
I Corinthians 12:9

This is not experimental or learned faith that we all get from hearing the Word (as it says in Romans 10:17), but the supernatural faith of God given for SPECIFIC circumstances. It is this faith that allowed Jesus to walk on the water, calm the storms, multiply food, and raise the dead.

We are always to work on developing REGULAR daily faith, because hearing the Word daily **and** doing the Word of God daily causes faith to grow (just as a muscle grows with use).

In the case of regular faith I believe that *faith won't add*. By this I mean that if you have half-enough faith to accomplish something, and I have half-enough faith to accomplish it, the sum total of the two half-faiths is still only half-enough faith. **Whoever has the greatest amount of faith in a group of believers has the highest level of faith that group can use.**

This supernatural *gift of faith* is the kind that Peter was given so he could walk on the water. However, even THAT kind of faith could not survive doubt. The minute PETER doubted, he sank. The Word says that even Jesus could not do miracles when surrounded with doubt.

> *"He* (Jesus) *did not many mighty works there because of their unbelief."*
>
> Matthew 13:58

Later, as we have already noted in detail above, supernatural faith was in operation in Peter's and Paul's lives.

It is a gift for any believer who wants it.

Gift(s) of Healing
I Corinthians 12:9

Notice that the word "gifts" is the only gift which is mentioned in the plural. These gifts cover so many areas that God distributed them individually to more than one person. I have observed that often a person has a part of this gift in that he or she may be effective in some kinds of healings, say backs and headaches, and another has more success with cancers and blood diseases. Thus with "gifts," all areas of healing are covered.

This is over and above the instructions to ALL believers in Mark 16, and in James where we are told to:

"call for the elders (mature ones), *and let them pray over him, anointing him with oil in the name of the Lord."*
James 5:14

Note that they were to call for the elders FIRST, not the doctors or the psychologists FIRST! How foolish we can be to get the pastor or the elders to come to the hospital **after the fact** when we could have called for the elders first, before stacking up hospital bills. If a miracle doesn't take place, THEN we can head for the doctors. They are wonderful backups. But let's work **first** at developing that faith.

How can God get the glory for what He says He loves to do, heal and deliver His people from evil, if we look for answers **elsewhere first?**

Working of Miracles
I Corinthians 12:10

This gift refers to **instant** healings, casting out of devils for physical healing (see Mark 9:14-29), opening blind eyes and deaf ears, loosing the tongue to speak, causing the lame to walk, restoring decayed teeth, etc. Some examples of miracles that were not healings are the multiplying of the loaves and fishes, and the calming of the winds and waves during a storm.

Prophecy
I Corinthians 12:10

This **gift of the Spirit** is not anointed preaching as if it were a talent, as some believe, but a prophetic gift used for edification, exhortation and comfort, as set forth in I Corinthians 14:3,

> *"But he that prophesieth speaketh unto men to edification, exhortation and comfort."*

This supernatural gift confirms things to a person that are unknown to anyone except God and the person to whom the prophecy is given. When this happens the person to whom the prophecy is directed sees that,

> *"... the secrets of his heart are made manifest, and so, falling down on his face he will worship God."*
>
> vs. 24,25

Prophecy can also reveal a person's future. While God strictly forbids coveting, He DOES instruct you to *"covet to prophesy"*(39). The **gift** of prophecy is not to be confused with the **office** of a prophet. One who prophesies is not necessarily a prophet. One is a gift to a man, the other is a gift to the church.

Discerning of Spirits
I Corinthians 12:10

This gift is for one purpose only: **to find (perceive or recognize) evil spirits.** This gift is closely tied to the ministry of casting out devils because you cannot cast them out if you cannot find (perceive or recognize) them.

Caution! There is a teaching that this gift enables a Christian to determine what spirit (Godly, Satanic, or fleshly) a person speaks by. **This is a misnomer**, and will be discussed further in Chapter Six.

Different Kinds of Languages
I Corinthians 12:10

This is not hocus-pocus mumbling or meaningless words. Webster's Dictionary defines "tongue" as a language or dialect.

While this gift is listed last in the passage, it was not done so because it was the least of the Gifts. If this were true, then in the "love chapter" (I Corinthians 13:13), where love is said to be **greater** than faith and hope, then love would also be deemed the least of the fruit of the Spirit, just because it is listed last. Of course we know that is not so.
"now faith, hope, love abide, these three BUT THE GREATEST OF THESE IS LOVE."

I Corinthians 14:2 says that if you speak in a tongue (a language you did not mentally learn or understand) you speak *"not unto men, but unto God."* This is certainly NOT a gift to be considered least! Also, *"He that speaketh in an unknown language edifies himself"* (vs. 4). Operating in the fullness of the Spirit is contingent upon being in communion with God and becoming all you can be through the power of the Spirit. If the church as a whole grasped this principle, and made sure it was **constantly edified, we would see much more being accomplished by God.**

I believe this gift refers to one of more than five thousand presently used languages in the world today. An example of this GIFT in operation was related to me by a pilot friend.

He flew a missionary-pastor to the interior of Bolivia, South America. He and the missionary attended a prayer meeting with native Bolivian Indians. During worship, one native was speaking perfect English. After the service, he went to the native to converse with him, and found that he could not speak one word with his own mind in English. That Indian's "unknown tongue" in which he prayed was English.

This gift isn't to enable us to speak another language just when we need to minister to someone who doesn't speak our language. On my three trips to Nigeria, West Africa, I would have appreciated the ability to speak to the natives without the necessity of an interpreter. However, even though I speak in tongues, I had to use an interpreter.

Speaking in tongues can take three different forms:

1.) **That which you speak when you are first filled** with the Holy Spirit (see Acts 10:46, and 19:6), unless you prophesy.
2.) **That which you speak supernaturally during a service.** This message from God needs to be interpreted so others can understand (see vs. 5). This is a gift, but not the gift of tongues described below.

3.) **The gift of tongues** (many times received at the time of being initially FILLED with the Holy Spirit), which then enables you **to speak it daily** from then on at your choosing, for your own personal edification.
    Of the nine spiritual gifts, this one is for you individually. The other eight are for the Church. Ask God

for it because it is so valuable. Otherwise how can you fulfill Jude's exhortation,

"But ye, beloved, building up your most holy faith, praying in the Holy Ghost . . . "

Jude 1:20

Paul told the believers that he wished they **all** spoke in tongues (their unlearned foreign languages), or prophesied.

"I would that ye all spoke in tongues rather that ye prophesy: for greater is he that prophesieth than he that speaketh with tongues (except he interpret that the church may receive edifying.)"

I Corinthians 14:5

So for your personal communication tongues are needed, and in church an interpreter is needed also.

There are those who do not understand this, who are offended to hear tongues spoken in a church, and even leave in the middle of a service upon hearing them. But why would Paul give such clear-cut instructions on when and how to speak in tongues if they were not important? I know of no one who would complain to hear a Spanish or Japanese person speaking in their foreign tongues, so, why should anyone complain if the same thing is done led by the Spirit, instead of learned with the mind? Would you? Of course not! **Let the Bible and the Spirit be our teachers, not denominational doctrines!**

When you are troubled by a matter your mind cannot understand, and you are at a loss on how to pray with your mind, the Spirit will help you pray as you speak in your Spirit-given language (that's why it is a **gift,** remember?).

" ...the Spirit helps our human weakness; for we know not how to pray as we ought."   Romans 8:26

When you pray a memorized prayer, or read one from a book, the prayer may not have any value as far as meeting a need, which is why Jesus condemned repetitious words when He taught,

> *"But when you pray, do not use vain* (i.e. "empty")*repetitions like unbelievers do; for they think that they shall be heard for their much speaking."*
>
> Matthew 6:7

However, when you pray in your other language (unknown to you), your mind is not involved. The Spirit can speak a perfect prayer **through** you, unhindered by your limited human mind, will or emotions.

Interpretation of Tongues
I Corinthians 12:10

This is when the Spirit gives an interpretation of the foreign language to someone who then speaks out the words of the Spirit in the understood language of the local church. This is a **gift to edify and encourage the church.**

The interpretation is not usually word for word, just as when you hear someone translate a speech he interprets the concepts to get the best meaning. This is why you will hear some interpretations being longer or shorter than the message. Languages vary so much that it often takes more or fewer words in one language to get the true meaning of the other.

Christians, the Gifts we have just covered are for the Church TODAY! God has put them in the Church for our growth. The Word *does not indicate anywhere* that God ever removed them. And if HE didn't, **we need to be extremely cautious** about dismissing them in our own churches.

Chapter Three
Hindrances to Church Growth

The operations of these gifts should be COMMONPLACE in your Spirit-led experience. Unfortunately they have become quite UNcommon.

Perhaps we have sought the infilling of the Spirit but have not gone on to pursue walking in the operation of these gifts. That would be seeking the blessing without being willing to be a blessing to others.

Or, perhaps we sought the Gifts without seeking the GIVER. God wants a PERSONAL relationship with His creations, and will not give **His gifts** to those who don't want **Him** *more than they want gifts*.

Or, perhaps there hasn't been a clear teaching on whether people were getting filled with His Spirit or simply just "getting a prayer language" (an unscriptural term).

Maybe church leaders feared offending those who have been taught that the infilling of the Holy Spirit happened at the time of their water baptism or conversion (see Acts 19:1).

Whatever the problem **has** been, **any** Godly leader can take the Word of God and correct the problem, either in themselves, and/or their people. In order for any move of God to be successful, it needs to come from God *through the leaders and pastors* to the congregations. If it does not, it will be stopped somewhere up the line as leaders rebel against this desire in their people. The Charismatic movement didn't have the staying power that the Pentecostal Movement did because the enthusiasm in the Spirit came **up** from the people, not

down from the leaders who watered it down, or stopped it.

Another problem is in trying to compare your own experience with that of another successful-looking ministry. God is such a personal God that He works with our **own** personalities. We must not judge ourselves by what others seem to be doing.

We never want to judge others by their outward appearance, as we do not want others to judge us. However, **we must discern wisely** as we choose where to go to church and what to believe.

Opportunists

A group that I label "opportunists" appear to be valid churches, but by closer observation, seem to be geared to impress men instead. Be very careful of impressive building programs, funded by "your" money, which end up financing grand, expensive architectural dreams.

I cannot tell you how often I find sick, broken and bondage-ridden people in the leadership positions of "successful" churches, knowing all the while that the Word says that signs, wonders and miracles of healing and deliverance **should be** following them instead. How can they be giving **victorious life** to the people if they do not have the answers for themselves?

"They shall cast out devils, speak with new tongues... lay hands on the sick, and they shall recover."

Is this what you see in the large congregations of the huge churches admired by the overall Christian community where you are? Some are. But sadly, most aren't.

Our decision about where to worship Him may appear to

be a matter of personal human choice. But it is not just a human choice if you want God's best. For He says,

"He that worships God MUST worship Him in Spirit and in truth."

John 4:24

According to the above mentioned Scripture I either worship God HIS way, or I'm not really worshiping Him at all. Why else would He have said it?

When we look at the examples of the seven types of Churches, described for us in the Book of Revelation, we can see, not only

1.) the **geographical** Churches of the New Testament, and
2.) the **characteristics** of the Church changes down the ages as they occurred, but also
3.)the **personalities of our Last Day churches** as they exist today just before His promised return.

Read about them in Revelation for yourself (Chapters 2 and 3) and with the help of the Holy Spirit, our teacher, see if you cannot see the great similarity between its prophecy about the Laodicean Church (the last one) and the worldwide Church's present-day condition.

*"And unto the Church of the Laodiceans write; these things saith the Amen, the faithful and true witness, the beginning of the creation of God, 'I know thy works, that thou art neither cold nor hot. So then, because thou art lukewarm, and neither cold nor hot, I will spew thee out of my mouth. Because thou sayest, **I am rich and increased in goods and have need of nothing,** and knowest not that thou art wretched, and miserable, and poor, and blind, and naked, I counsel you to buy of me **gold tried in the fire,** that thou mayest be rich; and **white raiment***

that thou mayest be clothed, and that the shame of thy nakedness do not appear; and anoint thine eyes with eyesalve, that thou mayest see."

This Scripture describes the spiritual condition of the **Church as a whole** today, NOT the **true remnant Church** that is fighting to stay true to its Calling, as Jesus said it would be.

Rich buildings with big debts are not what **God** is looking for, but for dedication, holiness, commitment to His way (not ours) with His Word as our guide.

"Let everything be done decently and in order."
I Corinthians 14:40

I Corinthians 14:40 was Paul's admonition to **God's order**, not man's. It's God's "gold tried in the fire" of life as you obey His Word, even though people will persecute you for it, that brings **His order.**

It's GOD's *"white raiment"* of real honest holiness before Him, and consistency in His Word with *"eyesalve"* to see and walk in the Gifts, that brings Him glory.

Let's go get it done, true Church! Let's start again! And this time, let's take that one other unifying step that was seen in the New Testament Church: i.e. the church in each city was called "the church at Ephesus," or "the church at Corinth." Our denominational lines should be replaced by an emphasis on our relationship to Jesus. I would like to see all fundamental churches called **"the Church at** (the name of your city), **the Baptist branch,"** or, **"the Church at** (the name of your city), the Full Gospel branch."

Our Biblical similarities, not our differences, should be emphasized. **We should be sharing our strengths with one another, not pointing out each others' weaknesses.**

Chapter Four
Getting Back to Basics:
Jesus As the Way

Salvation... born again... new birth... conversion... saved. These are words used to indicate what **Jesus** was talking about to Nicodemus when He said, "except a man be born again, he can NOT see the kingdom of God." Paul tells us in Romans 10:9 that, 1.)*"If we confess with our mouths that Jesus is Lord, and"* 2.) *"believe in our hearts that God raised Him from the dead,"* THEN we **are** saved.

This was **elementary teaching in the early church.** Yet today we have several major denominations that don't teach this true salvation to their congregations. Therefore, if people are saved in those particular denominations, it is by the grace of God, in spite of the church doctrine.

Salvation is the foundation and backbone of the church. **Without salvation, you are** *not a part of the church.* You may belong to a certain group and worship in their building, and may even think of yourself as a Christian; but, if **Jesus** has not become the CENTER of your existence because of your new understanding of how He loved you and had to die for you to make you right with God, and unless you have given **Him (not an organization)** the total right to your life, then *you do not have salvation* yet.

One of the common misconceptions in America is, that if you are not associated with one of the pagan religions, (i.e., not a Buddhist or an Muslim) then you are automatically a Christian. **I frequently ask people if they are Christians.** I get answers like, "No, I'm a Catholic," or, "No, I'm a Mormon," or, "I'm a Christian Scientist," or, "I'm a Congregationalist," or, "I'm a Baptist." This ONLY tells me where they go to church. It does not tell me **if** they are saved. Upon further conversation I found some had a personal relationship with Jesus, and some didn't.

Of the many different churches in existence today, if the one you attend believes in **Jesus'** salvation through **His** sacrifice as **He** stated it in **HIS** written Word , then it **is** a part of the true Church. It isn't enough to JUST believe in God. The Word says,

"Thou believest there is one God? Thou doest well, the devils also believe in God, and they tremble."

James 2:19

They, like many who call themselves Christians, do not understand that you can't know God except through a personal relationship with Jesus Christ.

Before going on to read what the future holds for Christians, perhaps you need to stop here and question whether you have been born again. If you are unsure, the Appendix found at the end of the last chapter of this book will help you determine where you stand in God's family. I encourage you to read over the material and take the steps necessary if you still are NOT **sure** of your own salvation.

Becoming part of the family of God has its basis in Scripture. **However, it is hidden in plain sight.** It is of such great importance that no church goer should stop searching until they find it. *He promises to show those who search for it with all their hearts.*

Without Jesus, it may be easy to agree with those who believe that a man lives and dies as animals do. One might believe that death is the end of existence or that people are reincarnated, coming back as another person or animal to begin life all over again. **None of these beliefs are true.** The Apostle Paul said that to be absent from the body is to be present with the Lord.

> *"Therefore we are always confident, knowing that, whilst we are at home* (i.e.,"comfortable") *in the body, we are absent from the Lord, (for we walk by faith, not by sight). We are confident, I say, and willing rather to be absent from the body, and to be present with the Lord."*
>
> II Corinthians 5:8

He understood that man was not just flesh and blood, but that he is primarily a **spirit.** The spirit of a man never dies, but his **flesh does** and is temporarily deposited in the ground to be resurrected and united again with our own spirits, just as Jesus' was.

Remember, His **spirit** left His body in the tomb while He retrieved the Old Testament saints from Paradise, also called Abraham's Bosom (their holding place). Then **He re-joined His body** to empower it into a "new" resurrected, glorified body.[4] Then He went to Heaven in the Ascension.

If we die before the rapture, our bodies stay in the earth, and our spirits will go to Heaven to be with the Lord (*to be absent from the body is to be present with the Lord*). At the Rapture, Jesus will come back first to get the bodies of those who are dead-in-Christ and re-unite them with their spirits which have been in Heaven (which is just a holding place for New Testament believers, as Paradise was a holding place for Old Testament believers.) Look at these Scriptures. Jesus

---

[4] 1 Peter 3:19, Eph. 4:8, Lk. 16:23

explained very plainly that resurrection will take place.

> *"Marvel not at this: for the hour is coming, in which all that are in the graves shall hear His voice and shall come forth; they that have done good unto the resurrection of life; and they that have done evil unto the resurrection of damnation."*
>
> John 5:29

The **Christian's resurrection** takes place at Christ's return to earth. He is judged innocent of sin by the Blood of the Lamb which paid the price for our sin.

> *"For if we believe that Jesus died and rose again, even so them also which sleep in Jesus will God **bring with Him**, and this we say unto you by the Word of the Lord, that we which are alive and remain until the coming of the Lord shall not precede them which are asleep, for the Lord Himself shall descend from heaven with a shout, with the voice of the archangel, and with the trump of God, and the dead in Christ shall rise first. And we which are alive shall be caught up **together** with them in the clouds, to meet the Lord in the air, and so shall we ever be with the Lord."*
>
> I Thessalonians 4:14-17

The **non-Christian's resurrection** doesn't take place for another 1,000 years after that time.

> *"... and they (true believers) lived and reigned with Christ a thousand years. But the rest of the dead lived not again until the thousand years were finished."*
>
> Revelation 20:4b,5

> *"...and I saw the dead, great and small, stand before God, and the Books were opened and the dead were judged out of those things written in the Books, and they were judged everyone according to their works, and death and hell*

were cast into the lake of fire."

Revelation 20:12,14

The non-Christian is resurrected to stand before God, who will judge him guilty, and cast him into the Lake of Fire. This eternal hell was not intended to be the final abode of man. **It was prepared for the devil and his fallen angels.** Man, in his disobedience and ignorance, has indicated to God that that is where he wants to go. I am sure you have come across the statement that God is Love, and He wouldn't send anyone to hell. It IS true that

> *"The Lord is not slack concerning His promise, as some count slackness: but is long-suffering toward us, **not willing that ANY should perish**, but that ALL should come to repentance."*

II Peter 3:9

But **people go to hell by their own choice** *not to want Him on earth*, so why would they want Him later? God has made available Heaven or Hell, blessings or cursings, and we are told to choose. He will not force us, or we would just be mindless puppets. Hell was not made for people. Again, it was created to hold the Devil and his angels. Jesus said,

> *"Then shall He say unto them on the left hand, 'Depart from me, ye cursed, into everlasting fire PREPARED FOR THE DEVIL AND HIS ANGELS.'"*

Matthew 25:41

And Isaiah 5:14 says,

> *"Therefore hell hath enlarged HERSELF, and opened her mouth without measure, and their glory, and their multitude, and their pomp, and he that rejoiceth shall descent into it."*

Notice that GOD did not make it bigger to accommodate

humans; **they did it themselves** by the large multitude of people who chose to go there. Heaven is where God intended us to go and be with Himself, and He told us how we can get there. That's only fair.

The only way to Heaven, regardless of what you may have been incorrectly taught, is through Jesus Christ, the Door. There simply **is no other way.** In John 14:6,

> *"Jesus saith unto Him, I am the Way the Truth and the Life. No man cometh unto the Father but by Me."*

From this passage, you can understand that knowing **about** God is not sufficient. God has put the entrance to Heaven into the hands of Jesus. **Knowing** Jesus personally is the *only way.*

People remark that so-and-so is such a good, moral person, and surely they are bound for Heaven. Unfortunately, good, moral people go to hell. Righteous people go to heaven, and it is not **their own** rightness that gets them there; it's the rightness **of Jesus.** It is in knowing HIM, and believing that *He is right* that gets us into Heaven.

God has great things planned and promised for the true Christian. Our lives here on earth are **just to prepare us** for greater, unending lives with God. God is trying to re-establish that unending relationship with man that He had intended to have with Adam before he sinned.

God came down to the Garden of Eden every evening to walk and talk with His Creations. There was nothing hindering that relationship.

But after Adam disobeyed God, he couldn't return to the Garden because Adam's sin separated him from God. Now He had to get rid of that barrier Adam had created between them, because Adam couldn't get rid of it by himself. God initiated animal sacrifices as the way for man to be reunited with God. The blood containing the life of the animal was offered to pay for that sin to remove that barrier.

These sacrifices continued for more than a thousand years until **Jesus became the** *total and last sacrifice* for mankind's sin, by sacrificing Himself on the cross to reunite man with His Father. That close relationship could then form again between God and men, *just as it had been in the Garden Of Eden.* It was **their** plan: God the Father's and God the Son's. They did it together. They were willing to do it because they loved their creations so much.

So the work that Jesus was to do had already started in the first few chapters of Genesis. **That work will be totally completed after Jesus comes back to earth in person again.** His return is mentioned in the Bible over 1400 times. Those who understand about His return are looking forward to it, and will see Him when He comes. He said He was coming for those who are looking for Him. If you haven't been taught that He is returning, and you are not a Christian desiring to see Him, He is not coming for you.

> *"Looking for and hastening unto the coming of the day of God..."*
>
> II Peter 3:12

That is a strong statement. From the beginning of time, God *The Father* established that only Jesus *His Son* would provide the way to reach Heaven.

Every believer should read the whole Bible **for themselves** because it is through reading the WORD of God *for yourself* that strong faith comes. But here it is for the time being in a nutshell.

God's Plan For Creation

Briefly, God's plan has unfolded through Earth's history just as He said it would. God has overseen His chosen ones, beginning with Abraham, God's designated "Father" of the Jewish nation, and his son, Isaac, and his grandson, Jacob. Because of famine, God sent Jacob's family South to Egypt to live there until rain came again to their homeland, Canaan (present-day Israel). God had one of Jacob's sons, Joseph, sold as a slave into bondage by his own brothers. Through God's direction, Joseph rose in power in that foreign land to become second only to Pharaoh in all of Egypt. God had placed him there to protect His people through the seven years of famine coming on the earth. These Israelites who came to Egypt at Joseph's invitation became a nation of almost one million people. They were established into twelve tribes after God delivered them out of Egypt's overbearing hand of slavery four hundred years later. On their way back to their promised land, Israel, they wandered around for forty years and then finally took back that land, the land of their forefathers.

God said that THESE people, Abraham's descendants, were HIS people; not the Chaldeans, the Syrians, the Romans, the Egyptians or the Arabs. (The Arabs were descendants of Abraham's OTHER son who married an Egyptian woman and produced the tribes of the Arabs.) From this union of God and the Jewish nation came a people who were referred to by God as His wife.

"For thy Maker is thine husband, the Lord of Hosts is His name: and thy redeemer the Holy One of Israel."

Isaiah 54:5

"Turn oh backsliding children, for I am married unto you."

Jeremiah 3:14

Jesus, in turn, is to be married to His bride, which is the true Christian Church. This is what is meant when the Scripture says that Jesus is coming back for His Church.

The Bible clearly states over and over that Jesus will return. In Acts 1, after Jesus' resurrection, as He was speaking to His followers, He was taken up into a cloud. And while they watched Him disappear, two angels stood by them and asked them why they were gazing into Heaven. **The angels said that Jesus would come back in this same way He left.** Also, in I Thessalonians 4:16, we are told,

> " *For the Lord Himself shall descend from heaven with a shout, with the voice of the archangel, and with the trump of God, and the dead in Christ shall rise first. Then we which are alive and remain shall be caught up together with them in the clouds, to meet the Lord in the air; and so shall we ever be with the Lord.* "

This event is often referred to today as *"The Rapture,"* although this word is not found in the Bible. These passages are most frequently read at funerals, and it is easy to consider them only as comfort for the mourners.

However, all saved mankind should be comforted by these words. This day spoken of here is almost at hand. When we understand this, it is only natural to begin to wonder, "Who is really going? **Am I?**" This is good reflection so that we keep clear **who it is** He said He would be coming for.

He died on the cross to make a bridge between God and man, re-opening the pathway that had been destroyed by man's sin. Those who have appropriated that sacrifice for their own sin, are now clean before God, and are now **referred to** *by Him* as kings and priests unto Him.

"You are a ROYAL PRIESTHOOD..."   I Peter 2:9

"Unto Him that loved us, and washed us from our sins in His own blood, and hath made us kings and priests unto God ..."

Revelation 1:6b-7

THIS is why God saved His people. It was not just so that you may have an escape from hell or have fire insurance. It was because He wants His people to rule and reign like kings (i.e., physical) **and priests** (i.e., spiritual) **with Him forever.**

"And I saw thrones, and they sat upon them, and judgment was given unto them, and I saw the souls of them that were beheaded for the witness of Jesus and for the Word of God, and which had not worshipped the beast, neither had received his mark upon their foreheads, or in their hands, and they lived and reigned with Christ a thousand years"

Revelation 20:4

So you and I (the Church) are expected to be ruling and reigning over Satan's powers of sin and sickness NOW. We are to PREVENT demonic powers from reigning rampant over our Earth FIRST. THEN we will know how to rule and reign with Him when He reigns from His throne in the restored temple in Jerusalem at His return. He is not coming back for a Church that has had no experience in ruling and reigning on earth! **This everyday abiding with Him in order to hear His commands** is our training ground. We're not just waiting helplessly to have Him finally jump in and save us. He HAS saved us! And we are to be ruling and reigning with the truths He gave us to do it with.

Jesus compared His return to that of a man who went on a journey and left his servants *in charge* of running his estate, telling the porter to watch. This man said that the porter needed to be vigilant in his watch so that the master of the house wouldn't come back and catch him sleeping. Are you sleeping? Are you watching?

With that same sense of urgency, I say to you, **Church, watch!** You must be looking for Him, not merely acknowledging that He may come at some future time. Peter tells us that Jesus' return will be like a thief in the night. If you know someone is coming, you will be prepared.

By the same token, we know that Jesus IS coming, and therefore our watch should be diligent, so that, when He returns, we are doing the works of God: i.e., telling the gospel with signs, wonders and miracles, *"the work of faith with power"* (II Thessalonians 1:11). Kings and priests are distinguished because of the obvious POWER they have in their lives that others around them don't have.

Jesus spoke of that time just prior to His return as a time of trouble on earth such as no man had ever seen. And the Book of Revelation tells us that a great portion of the world will be destroyed and millions of people will die in the first series of plagues scheduled to come upon the earth. Those Christians who miss The Rapture will be martyred in that period of time when the anti-Christ will rule on earth. **There won't be any buying or selling during this time without taking and showing the mark of the beast.**

> *"Let him that hath understanding count the number of the beast: for it is the number of a man, and his number is Six hundred threescore and six."*
>
> Revelation 13:18

All mankind will be forced to take this number (666) in order to participate in the one-world economic system. **True believers are warned not to take it or they will miss Heaven.**

> *"If any man worship the beast and his image, and receive His mark on his forehead, or in his hand, the same shall*

drink of the wine of the wrath of God and shall be tormented with fire and brimstone..."

Revelation 14:9-12

In order to be part of The Rapture, something is required of every true Christian. **Each one must be believing the Word of God and DOING it.** I am concerned about the teaching that everybody is automatically taken off the earth by the Lord. Some churches teach that being included in The Rapture is automatic, saying that all one needs to do is become saved, and when the Lord comes, you will automatically be taken away while the earth is purged with fire and other catastrophes. Not true. Jesus said,

*"**Be careful** or your hearts will become weighed down with dissipation, drunkenness and the stresses of life, and that day will close on you unexpectedly. For as a snare shall it come on all them that dwell on the face of the whole earth. WATCH THEREFORE, and pray always that you **may be accounted worthy to escape** all these things that shall come to pass, and to stand before the Son of man."*

Luke 21:34-36

This does not sound automatic does it?

I John 2:28 states,

*"And now little children, **abide in Him** (Jesus) that when He shall appear we may have confidence and not be ashamed before Him at His coming."*

Abide in Him. This doesn't mean giving mental assent to His existence, or abiding often in your church building. It means having **your whole being so totally, daily in tune with Him that you are not surprised or ashamed at His coming because you ARE doing His work.** If you are ashamed at His coming, it will indicate that you hadn't been abiding in Him before His coming. In Revelation 3:3, Jesus admonished the early church to remember what they had heard and to

*"Hold fast and repent if therefore thou shall **not** watch, I will come on thee as a thief, and thou shall **not** know what hour I shall come upon you."*

Notice that it says if you don't watch, you won't know. On the other side, it you do watch, *you will* know. Jesus' response to his disciples when they asked Him when He was coming back again was that, at *that time,*

"No man knows (present tense)*the hour."*

John 14:16

However, from further Scripture, which they hadn't yet received at that time, we find that we **WILL** know, for it says,

*"For when they say, 'Peace and safety!' then sudden destruction cometh upon them, as travail upon a woman with child; and they shall not escape. **But ye, brethren, are not in darkness that that day shall overtake you as a thief.** Ye are the children of light, and the children of the day: we are NOT of the darkness. Therefore let us not sleep as others do; but let us WATCH and BE ALERT."*

I Thessalonians 5:3-6

Let me interject here that **the world is presently looking for a Savior.** NOT Jesus as Savior, but a man who can pull the world out of the present problems it faces.

We have worldwide financial problems and there are those who say a **"one-world order" will solve that.** The man in charge of this "one-world order" will emerge publicly in the world news and be recognized as its "savior." He shall have the answer for the impending chaos and pull the nations together under his one-world government for a short period of time, until Jesus puts an end to his rule.

He will appear to be peace-loving in the beginning, but is unbelievably wicked underneath, and able to turn men from trusting the Lord, to trusting himself. Some thought Hitler or Mussolini was he. But they did not even come close to causing world peace.

Remember the above Scripture which says people will be saying, "*Peace and safety!*" **We'd better not be deceived by this, Church,** but, as the Word of God warns, "*Watch and be alert!*"

Watch for that Man of Sin and the prophesied signs that will surround him, i.e., wars and turmoil will cease. The Word above said that when peace and safely are proclaimed, "*then sudden destruction.*"

This is speaking of the tribulation period discussed earlier. The Old Testament prophet, Amos, also said,

> "*Surely the Lord God will do nothing, but he revealeth his secrets unto his servants the prophets.*"
>
> Amos 3:7

This is why you need to become a Christian, to be a servant of God **to rule and reign with Him in the near future**, not just to get to Heaven.

Heaven, as it exists today, is not our final destination anyway. Most people think that after you have lived and died (if you were good) you go to Heaven. This is a misunderstanding. We are going to Heaven only long enough for the world to be cleaned up and made properly fit for our presence again. Revelation says that *after fire cleans the earth of pollution and sin*, then a **New Heaven** and a **New Earth** are ruled over by Christ and US.

"And I saw a new heaven and a new earth; for the first heaven and the first earth were passed away, and there was no more sea."

Revelation 21:1

The earth will be rejuvenated, sin will be gone, and God will reign through **Jesus Christ with us who return from heaven to earth with Jesus after the marriage supper of the Bride and the Lamb.**

"And I, John, saw the Holy City, new Jerusalem, coming down from God out of heaven prepared as a bride adorned for her husband."

Revelation 21:2

The Bible is so full of such exciting information that, as Christians **read** the Word, they find out there are exciting days ahead. The Church is going to be restored **as** we rule and reign with Him as we Christians finally take our proper place of authority on this earth. The devil is presently "the prince" of the power over the earth. But ONLY the PRINCE. We are KINGS and we can put the evil prince under our authority, just as Jesus, our King, did when He was on earth .

We have seen in this chapter that the real Bride of Christ is:

1.) intently watching for Christ to return,

2.) consistently abiding personally with Christ daily, and

3.) walking in power.

Does this describe your daily experience? If not, it could be because the source of power, His Holy Spirit, is missing in your life.

Take heart, dear Church, and read on.

Chapter Five
The Holy Spirit:
The Source of the Power

Before Jesus' death on the cross, He warned His disciples that He was going to go away, and that frightened them. He comforted them with the assurance that, although He had many things to teach them which they could not yet understand, when the Holy Spirit came HE would comfort them and guide them into **all** truth.

"Nevertheless, I tell you the truth; it is expedient for you that I go away; for if I go NOT away, the Comforter will not come unto you; but if I depart, I will send him unto you."

*"**He** will guide you into all truth, for he shall not speak of Himself, but whatsoever he shall hear, that shall he speak, and he will show you things to come."*

John 16:7,13

These men were already believers, and knew the gospel. But they would need supernatural wisdom above and beyond their own understanding to do His work on earth after He left.

Then, again, after Jesus arose from the dead and spent forty days teaching them just before He ascended to Heaven where He is now, He told them to wait in Jerusalem until they were filled with power (divine ability) from on high.

"And, being assembled together with them, He commanded them that they should not depart from Jerusalem, but wait for the promise of the Father, which, saith He, you already heard of Me. For John truly

baptized with water; but ye shall be baptized with the Holy Ghost not many days from now."

Acts 1:4,5

"But ye shall receive power after the Holy Spirit has come upon you."

Acts 1:8

Do you see how Jesus said it twice just before He left them? They were to wait in Jerusalem until they were filled with power so that they would not go try to save the world without it. This power was to come from the HOLY SPIRIT **himself. Not an "it" but a person, him** (see all the "he's" in John 16 quoted above). The Bible refers to the Holy Spirit as a Teacher, the Spirit of Truth, and a Comforter. He is, of course, one third of the God-head.

The Holy Spirit is not a "type of influence" from the Father. He is not the Spirit of the Father. Romans 8 teaches that God is a Spirit and has a spirit; Jesus is a spirit and has a spirit; and the Holy Spirit is a spirit and has a spirit.

"But you are not in the flesh but in the Spirit, if so be that the Spirit of God dwell in you. Now if any man have not the Spirit of Christ, he is none of his. And if Christ be in you, the body is dead because of sin: but the Spirit is life because of righteousness. But if the Spirit of Him who raised up Jesus from the dead dwell in you, he that raised up Christ from the dead shall also quicken your mortal bodies by his Spirit that dwelleth in you. Therefore, brethren, we are debtors, not to the flesh, to live after the flesh. For if ye live after the flesh, ye shall die; but if ye through the Spirit do mortify the deeds of the body ye shall live. For as many as are led by the Spirit of God, they are the sons of God."

Romans 8:9-14

This spirit of the Holy Spirit may dwell in a Christian and empower him to do things he couldn't do otherwise. So Jesus commanded the disciples to remain in Jerusalem and wait for the Holy Spirit. And what an experience they had when they did!

According to the account in Acts 1, they were all (one hundred and twenty of them) filled with the promised Holy Ghost and began to **speak fluently in languages they had not learned** as this Holy Spirit flowed through them.

There were many Jews in Jerusalem, on pilgrimages from every nation, celebrating the **Feast of Pentecost** which God had told them to do **every year** on the fiftieth day after the Feast of Firstfruits, since 1490 B. C. (Leviticus 23:15,16).

When these foreigners heard the hundred and twenty speaking about Jesus' good news **in their own native languages**, you can believe there was much excitement. The disciples were even accused of being drunk by those who didn't understand the languages and called it babbling. But Peter spoke up with a new boldness which the Holy Spirit had just given him, and said that this event was the one spoken of by the prophet Joel:

> *"It shall come to pass in the last days I will pour out my spirit on all flesh; and your sons and your daughters shall prophesy, your old men shall dream dreams, your young men shall see visions; and also upon the servants and upon the handmaids in those days will I pour out my spirit."*

Joel 2:28-29

People have interpreted this to mean that there will be a great last-days revival of new souls born into the Kingdom of God, but that is NOT what Joel said.

He said (prophetically) that in the last days God would pour out His spirit on **all** flesh. As you study this verse in context with the surrounding Scriptures, you will see that it is **not** talking about everybody accepting His newly poured-out Spirit, which would indeed be a great revival. But this end-time happening would make His Holy Spirit **available to everyone** for the first time in history: i.e., to **"all" types and classes**, even the lowest class of people. In the Old Testament the strict class structure kept "the servants and handmaidens" as the lowest forms of citizens. Therefore, Joel is prophesying that the Holy Spirit would no longer fall on just the seers, priests and the occasional king, but on the common people as well.

There are those who believe that the receiving of the Holy Spirit is an automatic thing which comes with our salvation experience. But Scripture clearly teaches this is not true. Let's look carefully at our Biblical examples.

Paul asked the **already born-again believers** in the Ephesus church,

> *"'Have ye received the Holy Ghost since you believed?'*
> *And they said unto him, 'We have not so much as HEARD whether there be any Holy Ghost.'*
> *And he said unto them, 'Unto what then were you baptized?'*
> *And they said, 'Unto John's baptism.'*
> *Then said Paul, 'John truly baptized with the baptism of repentance saying unto the people that they should believe on him which should come after him, that is on Christ Jesus.'*
> *When they heard this they were baptized in the name of the Lord Jesus, and when Paul had laid his hands upon them, the Holy Ghost came on them and they spoke with tongues and prophesied."*

Acts 19:2-6

This is the exact same thing that had happened on the Day of Pentecost when the original one hundred and twenty were filled, they spoke in tongues and prophesied.

On another occasion, a Gentile (i.e., non-Jewish) believer (Cornelius) was being taught by Peter, and while Peter was still speaking the Holy Spirit fell on **all** of them which heard the word (Acts 10:44). **They already were believers.** Those who were traveling with Peter were astonished because the Gentiles also received the gift of the Holy Ghost. (Up to that time the disciples had believed that only Jewish people were going to receive their own Messiah.) How did they know the Holy Ghost had fallen? It says,

> "...because on the Gentiles also was poured out the gift of the Holy Ghost for they heard them speak with tongues and magnifying God."
>
> (vs. 45-46)

And on yet another occasion some believers in Philip's church, in Samaria, *who had already been baptized*, and had witnessed many healings and deliverances, were visited by Peter and John from the Jerusalem church.

> "Now when the apostles which were at Jerusalem heard that Samaria had received the word of God, they sent unto them Peter and John, who, when they were come down, prayed for them, that they might receive the Holy Ghost, *(for as yet He was fallen upon none of them, only they were baptized in the name of the Lord Jesus).* Then they laid their hands on them and they received the Holy Ghost."
>
> Acts 8:14-17

It is also worthy to note here that in this same instance, a powerful, bewitching man wanted the power of the Holy Spirit and offered to pay the disciples for it after he had been born again.

How did he know they had received it? Because, it says, he

"saw that through the laying on of hands the Holy Ghost was given."

vs. 18

How many times do we need to see this happening *in our Scriptures which we say we believe* before we change "our" theology to fit the truth in the Word? It is very obvious that not ONLY did Jesus make his atoning power available to whosoever believed in Him, **but also told them to wait for the next available outpouring of His gifts.** *One is the experience of accepting His gift of love. The other is the experience of accepting His gift of power. Two experiences.*

Whether they come to you years apart, or minutes apart, is up to what you believe and receive. Jesus Himself was God, the Son of God, and yet the Holy Spirit did not come upon Him and em**power** Him for ministry until He was baptized by John. He did absolutely no miracles before that, because He did not have that power yet to minister with.

Many dear Christian people have loved God and obeyed Him to their deaths, yet diseases, and defeat beat them down to a pulp, and they ask, "Why does God allow this?" It is true that we are always going to have evil influences in varying degree, for God has made them part of the plan of earth because sin and demonic forces are everywhere. **But we, like His example of His life on earth showed us, are to have victories over them.** We are not only to be loving, patient and kind like Jesus, but strong and tough like Jesus against suffering and sickness as well. We must see His whole example of what we are to be, not just the part we find the easiest. **The more we see this in the Word, and know this in our hearts, the**

better we get at it.

So if you have not yet been filled with His Holy Spirit, get to someone who already has been filled in this Biblical way, agree with them over these Scriptures, have them lay hands on you as Peter and Paul did to believers, and expect to be filled! **"Receive the Holy Spirit"** is all they have to say with faith, and you WILL. It happens all the time in today's Christian world to those who have received the Full Gospel as you now have.

Scripture says,

"Jesus Christ, the same, yesterday, today and forever."
Hebrews 13:8

God said,

"I am the Lord, I change NOT."
Malachi 3:6

Therefore, the same ministry that Jesus imparted to the disciples should be seen today. We need that power because we aren't fighting **people**, but we are fighting spiritual **forces** of evil that try to keep us sinning against God. We are to put on the WHOLE armor of God, not just part of it. This armor comes from the Holy Spirit. Listen,

"Brothers, be strong in the Lord and the power of His might. Put on the whole armor of God that you may be able to stand against the wiles of the devil. For we wrestle not against flesh and blood, but against principalities, against powers, against the rulers of the darkness of this world, against spiritual wickedness in high places. Wherefore take unto you the whole armor of God that you may be able to withstand in the evil day, and having done all to stand!"
Ephesians 6:10-13

Then he emphasizes accepting the WHOLE, powerful truth of God, from your head to your toe, not just parts of it. Every bit of armor covered some part of the body.

God gave the church apostles, prophets, evangelists, pastors, and teachers for the PERFECTING of us saints, for the WORKING of the ministry, for the EDIFYING of the body of Christ(Ephesians 4:11). These ministry **gifts of the Holy Spirit** all work with this whole armor.

So if we truly want to become more PERFECT, or WORK in a ministry, or EDIFY the body of Christ (i.e., strengthen each other), there is only one way, *through the Holy Spirit.*

To believe that "the ministry of the person of the Holy Spirit in power is no longer necessary," as some religious institutions do, is to contradict God's Word. Throughout Scripture God was, and still is, a powerful "sign and wonder" God.

Jesus Himself was,

"approved of God among you by miracles, and wonders and signs which God did by Him in the midst of you."
Acts 2:22

Throughout the New Testament alone the phrase **"signs and wonders"** appears eighteen times in connection with God working with His people.

When Jesus commissioned the apostles, He told them to go into all the world and preach. He further told them that they had four ministries that they were to tend to: to heal the sick, cleanse the lepers, raise the dead, and cast out devils. **The need for those ministries still exists today.** Although our current worst disease is not leprosy, we still deal with serious sicknesses. Each generation has its own newest disease, no worse to us than leprosy was to them. There are new diseases appearing every year that doctors cannot diagnose or treat. Jesus commanded diseases to be healed and evil spirits to depart. He showed us how, and told us to do it the same as He did.

The field of parapsychology says that there are no evil spirits, yet psychologists cannot explain weird phenomena in people, calling them victims of drastic mental disorders. The worst of these dear, driven people are hidden away in mental hospitals. Jesus didn't skirt issues like that. He delivered them with power and compassion, and commanded us to do the same. **The need for believers who will walk in these powerful gifts of healing and delivering is still as great today as it ever was** (more about this in Chapter 8).

What is keeping the vast majority of the churches from experiencing this power? I believe some churches are waiting for God to do more, but God is waiting for us to believe the Word and do *our part*. **God has already done His part. He took away our sins, taught us, gave us His Word, His authority and His powerful Holy Spirit. Now He expects us to use our armor and go forward with it.**

There is no need to stop and fight over doctrine. When you walk in the power of God with signs, wonders and miracles, you PROVE you have the right doctrine! Fight the enemy, not each other!

Many churches have waited and waited for revival, not realizing what **true revival is. True revivals are revolutions. The force with which they come is in exact proportion to the light men receive. This light reveals bondages enslaving the church and the benefits denied the church through ignorance and tradition.**

Revolutionaries are people who have seen the truth in the

Scriptures, and demanded their rights as written in their Champions' Instruction Manual.

The American revolution was the same thing in the natural. Men realized that the Declaration of Independence gave them the right to be free of oppression, and they decided they were going to fight for their human rights. Equally, the Bible is the written will of the rights which God says belong to believers: health, peace, joy. We have the right to use the weapons of our warfare to fight the evil forces against us that keep us from being free from sin, sickness and death. *But we must know the power we have and how to use our weapons!*

True revivals require the responsibility of each individual to continuously know the Word, believe the Word, and fight the enemy. This is true revival though the power of the Spirit.

Those powerful gifts of the Holy Spirit, written in I Corinthians 12 (which I explained in Chapter Two), can ONLY come ONCE you have received the Holy Spirit. When He is received, He imparts these various gifts to you which are so necessary in the working of the church today.

Why do you think churches fight so much about the Holy Spirit as they do? Why do you suppose they have been ignorant of Him for so long? There can be only one answer: **The enemy of our souls is afraid that we will gain the same power and authority Jesus had over him!**

Satan tried his best to sway Jesus from doing the will of the Father. He trembles at the thought of the Church, Christ's Bride, understanding and receiving the Holy Spirit.

The mark of a successful church is not the size of its congregation, or how magnificent a building it has, or how large the denomination is that is backing it. *A church that can successfully bring the work of the enemy to a standstill through the power of the Holy Spirit and can set the captives free is a successful church.*

Now let's look at why "speaking in tongues" brings power. Why did God give us foreign languages to pray in?

Jude 20 says, *"But you, beloved, building up yourselves on your most holy faith, **praying in the Holy Ghost,** keep yourselves in the love of God, looking for the mercy of our Lord Jesus Christ unto eternal life."*

What does praying in the Holy Ghost mean? Paul explained it in I Corinthians 14:12-15,

*"... even so you, for as much as you are zealous of spiritual gifts, seek that ye may excel to the EDIFYING OF THE CHURCH. Wherefore let him that speaks in an unknown language pray that he may interpret. For if I pray in an unknown language my spirit prays, but my understanding is unfruitful. **I will pray with the spirit and I will pray with the understanding, also, I will sing with the spirit** and I will sing with the understanding also, else when you shall bless with the spirit how shall he that occupieth the room of the unlearned say Amen at the giving of thanks, seeing he understands NOT what you say? For thou verily givest thanks well, but the other is not edified. **I thank God I speak with other languages more than you all."***

How clear he makes it that we must pray *both ways*:

1.) without the mind's interference, in the Spirit, and
2.) with the mind, through our thinking process.

There are specific times, places and reasons for each way.

Paul was saying that he had the ability to speak in his unknown language OR speak in his native tongue. He could also sing either way. He did it, either in the language that other people understood so that they knew when to say "Amen!" to his giving of thanks, or in his unknown language which would build himself up in the Spirit, personally enabling him to pray correctly as the Spirit interceded for him.

Another Scripture dealing with this says that he who speaks in an unknown language edifies himself, and he that prophesies, (in his own known language) edifies the church (I Corinthians 14:4). Here we see both ways again.

I cannot overemphasize the necessity of laying aside whatever doctrine hinders you from receiving the Holy Ghost in His wonderful fullness. He can then work through you to complete the Church. Jesus cannot come back to earth until such time as the Church has been fully restored to its glorious place. That includes being filled with the Spirit and doing the works of God.

God has chosen to use us **humans** with all our imperfections, rather than the angels, to fulfill the spreading of the Word of God to all men. Only the Scripture's total (not partial) good news will lift the despair that many people suffer from. Depression and suicide are two of the greatest problems in our country. Both these problems can be overcome with the powerful help of the Holy Spirit. Let Him minister through you effectively.

Peter tells us that we are to

"Be sober and vigilant because your adversary, the devil, walks about like a roaring lion, seeking whom he may devour: whom you can resist in steadfast faith."

I Peter 5:8

This is **only intimidation** by the enemy. It does not say he IS a roaring lion. He only **imitates** one. We are to call his bluff, but this can only be done if we know the power that we have through the Holy Spirit. It is the Holy Spirit who shows you how and empowers you to resist the devil (James 4:7).

It is through the Holy Spirit that mighty truths are revealed to the believer in the very same way He revealed the truths about Jesus to the disciples after Jesus was gone (John 16:13). If you KNOW it is the TRUTH that "greater is He that is in you than he (the devil) that is in the world" (I John 4:4), **then** you can get power over the sins and sicknesses that he tries to lay on you. The Holy Spirit's presence in the life of the believer can change that person dramatically.

Notice once more, that the last instructions of Jesus are filled with commands to resist the devil's works:

"In my NAME shall they cast out devils, speak with new tongues, take up serpents, and if they drink any deadly thing it shall not hurt them, they shall lay hands on the sick and they shall recover."

Mark 16:17-18

These are all the very things He had already shown them how to do. He had said previously,

"The thief (enemy) comes to steal, kill and destroy, but I have come that you may have life, and life more ABUNDANTLY"

John 10:10

Now He expected them to do the same things He did **in "His NAME".** The word "name" means His same character and authority. Therefore, we are to be totally submerged (baptized) into the character and authority of the Father, the Son and the Holy Ghost. When we are, the devil recognizes

Jesus' authority within us, realizes he is defeated, and flees.

Sometimes a church teaches that the Holy Ghost falls on them afresh from Heaven. They refer to this as being "anointed," and then they "feel" empowered to do certain things for God. On the contrary, according to Romans 8, the Holy Spirit abides *within you*. He does not fall all over again from Heaven, but is stirred up within you.

> *"Ye are not in the flesh if so be that the **Spirit of God dwell in you.**"*
>
> Romans 8:9

> *"The anointing which you have received from Him abides **within** you."*
>
> I John 2:27

> *"Wherefore I put thee in remembrance that thou stir up the gift of God which is **in thee** by the laying on of my hands."*
>
> II Timothy 1:6

What had Paul given to Timothy by the laying on of hands? The baptism of the Holy Ghost!

You are empowered to do all this as a Christian once you are filled with the Holy Ghost. Let no man's doctrine keep you from receiving God's total best. The *full gospel* belongs to you.

What has happened to the Church? It has gone into a state of dormancy **within** those who will not go on to the *full truth*. God has not changed or left. The God-ordained ability of His Church has not lessened.

We have let the enemy convince us that we cannot do God's will, and allowed **men in leadership** to water down the Word of God to match their own human inadequacies. Only men's ignorance, complacency, traditions, or lack of understanding have allowed many of the precious things of God to fall away. In their place, we have put in doctrinal dogma rather than praise and worship and the moving of the powerful works of God as He instructed us to do.

Men and women of God, stand up and fight the good fight of faith! Renew your faith on **His** Word, not just on the words you have heard from others who may seem to know what they are talking about. Make Jesus' faith **your own**. How blessed Paul and Barnabus must have been when the people they came to in Berea listened to them and then *"they received the word with all readiness of mind, and searched the Scriptures daily, whether those things were so"* (Acts 17:11).

They took responsibility for their own faith. We must not blame any one for teaching us wrong. We all have Scriptures, and we can all be taught by and empowered by the Holy Spirit.

What could be holding you back?

Chapter Six
Ten Roadblocks on the Path
To Operating
in the Fullness of the Spirit

Roadblock Number One

"Then spake Joshua to the Lord in the day when the Lord delivered up the Amorites before the children of Israel and he said in the sight of Israel, 'Sun, stand thou still upon Gibeon, and thou, Moon, in the valley of Ajalon.'"

And the sun stood still, and the moon stayed, until the people had avenged themselves upon their enemies...

So the sun stood still in the midst of heaven and hasted not to go down about a whole day. And there was no day like that before it or after it, that the Lord hearkened to the voice of a man, for the Lord fought for Israel."

Joshua 10:12-14

First, Joshua spoke to God, then he **commanded** the sun to stand still, and so God hearkened to the voice of a man. Modern-day scientists have confirmed that this event actually took place in that the sun stood still in the skies. They confirm that there is a missing day somewhere in the technologically-computed count of days and masses in space.

The ability to incorporate supernatural power into our lives is clearly missing in these last days. Jesus **told** us that we would do greater things than He did,

"Verily, verily I say unto you, He that BELIEVETH in Me, the works that I do shall he do also, and GREATER

works than these shall he do, because I go unto my Father."

John 14:12

and that means **incorporating the supernatural into day-to-day living**. Do you have the faith to believe that the elements in the skies would obey you if you operated in enough Godly authority? God said,

"Ask of Me things concerning My sons, and concerning the work of My hands, command ye Me."
Isaiah 45:11

God Himself said to command Him regarding the work of His hands: the sun, moon and stars in this case. Joshua knew this when he commanded the sun to stand still. Elijah knew this too when he stopped the rain from falling for three years. Remember too, that "command" does *not mean*, "think it in your head somewhere," it means "**say it, out loud.**"

The key is that Joshua's faith had been exercised and increased over the years by serving God, so he knew that as he spoke out loud with authority, he would again see the supernatural.

He did not give up after a few times of trying. **He exercised that faith like a muscle.**

The **more** he used it, the **more** results he saw, the **more** he believed, the **more** faith that produced, the **more** he boldly spoke out loud with authority.

It is a *powerful pattern* that is God-ordained and will work for any man or woman who sees it!

Of course we **all** have fears that it will not work. Fear can be THE FIRST ROADBLOCK, but only if WE let it be. Keep your eyes on the pattern.

The enemy constantly lies to us that it will not work. God allows his deception so that we can make a choice. If that choice were not there, we would just be robots.

We have to know who fear comes from, recognize it when it is happening, refuse it, and believe God's promises for this *powerful pattern for success* .

The seed of faith was implanted into you at the moment you received your new birth.

"but think soberly (with sound thinking), *according as God hath dealt to every man THE measure of faith."*
Romans 12:3b

Roadblock Number Two

That **measure of faith** is the same measure for everyone in the infant stage of our salvation. From then on your faith enables you to use the authority given to you as a Spirit-filled believer, but **only if** you keep exercising it.

I've seen thousands of Spirit-filled believers over the years sitting in pews with the same little seed of faith that never grew because they **would** not exercise it. They loved to come to church and hear of others walking in the power, but became unable to master sin and sickness themselves, because they would not exercise their faith with authority in their homes. They had that measure of faith, but no authority.

Faith and authority are not the same thing. Faith comes when you're saved. Authority comes from the Holy Spirit when you are baptized in Him. Upon receiving the Holy Spirit, you receive the authority to USE the power. Jesus promised,

> *"But you shall receive POWER when the Holy Spirit comes upon you."*

Acts 1:9

That authority, however, needs to be increased with use continually.

Jesus told His followers, among other things, to cast out demons. We can do the same. But demons are not cast out unless authority is used. One can quote the Name of Jesus, which devils hate, but quoting the Name without the authority will not remove them. The demons said to someone using Jesus' Name, *"I know Jesus and I know Paul, but who are YOU?"* and that question, which says in essence, "Who do you think **you** are?" has to be answered with authority by a person who **knows their own power in Christ, and cannot be swayed by some demon suggesting you have none!**

You do have all the authority you need to cast out demons if you have the Holy Spirit residing within you. That authority, however, has to be increased continually with use. Not continuing to develop it by use would be a SECOND ROADBLOCK.

I like to compare this principle to the example of a law enforcement officer taking an average man off the street, giving him a badge, and telling him he is a policeman. He has had no training, no experience, and no chance to operate in the authority that has been thrust upon him. His first few weeks on the job would make him a nervous wreck. He has the authority to stop traffic and make arrests, and the public recognizes that fact, but any resistance of a criminal, or dangerous or violent situation, would jar his confidence quickly. He has to increase his confidence a step at a time, with experience. The authority is there but he has no real knowledge of its power.

So it is with us. We have the stamp of the Holy Spirit which is like that badge. The demons know it's there, but they will test it. And only as you keep on standing against them will they weary of your relentless faith-filled words and flee!

Roadblock Number Three

Also, you will discover that with use you will develop more authority **over some areas**, like cancers or back problems, before other areas, like migraine headaches and depression. This is because faith is not a blanket situation.

Just because you have developed authority in some areas doesn't mean you will have that same strength in other areas until you determine to develop them there as well. You may have faith to believe that the deaf can be healed, but lack the faith yet to believe that limbs can be restored. Picture a weightlifter with unlimited strength in his arms. Since the whole body is involved in weightlifting, he will need to exercise his leg muscles independently as well, in order to be all he can be as a contender.

So don't get stuck behind this THIRD ROADBLOCK of discouragement when not EVERYTHING is healed at the same rate of success in the beginning. *When you have done everything there is to do, stand, and stand again.*

Roadblock Number Four

A FOURTH ROADBLOCK is believing that the larger

the number of people in a prayer group, the more faith there is.

It has been my experience that two half-faiths do not make a whole faith. The highest level of the faith of a group is the person with the most faith there. Faith does not add. It was Jesus' faith that got people healed. When He said, *"Your faith has made you whole,"* it was their faith in HIS faith. *His* was the highest faith around.

To illustrate this, imagine that you are scaling Mt. Everest. You find, however, that you have only half-enough strength to reach the top. So you call someone else to help you who also has only half enough strength to reach the top. You would BOTH be stuck in the middle. If, however, you called someone who was strong enough to get you both to the top, he would meet you half way and carry you to the top. He wouldn't need you, but because of his excellent physical condition, you couldn't have finished the journey without him.

If climbing mountains is important to you, you will make a point of working daily at being in excellent physical condition. If doing the works of God is important to you, you will want to be in excellent spiritual condition. Use your faith first in areas where you feel most confident you will see results. Then expand your faith to **reach into situations that seem impossible. As you use that faith, it will grow** and people with smaller faith can count on you to take them higher.

Roadblock Number Five

When it comes to the area of casting out demons, there is a FIFTH ROADBLOCK which I have seen believers fall headlong into. And that is in thinking that this power-in-numbers theory works in deliverance from demons as well. *Not true.*

You can, with authority, command a demon to leave in Jesus' name, and it will. However, calling ten or twenty people to help you cast out that demon doesn't either improve your faith, or produce any more authority.

It is, in fact, counterproductive in that one person speaking with authority is much less confusing than twenty people commanding different things of the demon(s). Think, for instance, of a big German shepherd dog lying on a rug in front of the fireplace. His owner comes into the room and commands him to get back into the kitchen. I can see the dog responding to the authority and the simplicity of the master's command without any trouble. If, however, all six members of the family come into the room and begin giving different commands from all directions to the dog ("Get out of here!" "Go outside!" "Go to the kitchen!" "You don't belong here!" "Go to your box!") the dog would be hard pressed to know which command to obey.

In the beginning of our deliverance ministry many years ago, I believed, as many did, that loudness and numbers were more effective than just one person ministering. We discovered that not only did we confuse the demons that way, but that they used it against us as well, asking us different questions, confusing and intimidating US (see more details in the next chapter). **We discovered with experience that calm steady authority by one person with faith in his or her ministry got the job done much more effectively.** I still deliver people from demons with those same, calm, strong commanding words that Jesus used. You can do the same because Jesus did it that way. I just instruct those around me to softly praise God or pray in their prayer language by the Spirit.

Roadblock Number Six

THE SIXTH ROADBLOCK is believing that doubt only slightly hinders faith's power. Wrong!

The effect of doubt on your faith is staggering. Consider the time when Jesus Himself could not do any mighty work in his home town because of their doubt.

> *"And He could do no mighty work there, save that he laid his hands upon a few sick folk, and healed them. And he marvelled at their unbelief. And he went around the villages teaching."*

Mark 6:5,6

Why? Because DOUBT is not the same as LACK OF FAITH. If this were so, unconscious people would not be healed. They had no lack of faith. They just didn't have the power of doubt. **Doubt is an active power.** Lack of faith is just a neutral emptiness, and does not hurt.

When Jesus was about to raise Jairus' daughter from the dead he made the doubters leave (Luke 8:49-56).

> *"They laughed him to scorn, knowing she was dead, and he put them all out, and took her by the hand and called, saying, 'Maid, arise.'"*

Luke 8:53,54

Obviously Jesus had total faith but the doubt of the people affected his actions. When Peter walked on the water toward Jesus, he started to sink only after he saw the size of the waves. Doubt crept in. Jesus knew the problem immediately and said, *"Why do you doubt?"* **So get rid of the doubters when you're about to do serious praying or standing in agreement for God's**

promises!

Roadblock Number Seven

The SEVENTH ROADBLOCK can occur when you confuse hope with faith. **Hope is not faith.**

Have you sought things from God, presuming that you had the faith to believe Him for those things, and later looked back and realized that you had doubts? This is because you hoped for something instead of having real faith.

To remedy this situation you must know what real faith is and how to get it.

*"Faith is the **substance** of the things hoped for, the evidence of things not seen yet."*
Hebrews 11:1

Faith is a substance, something concrete. It is the written promise of God. It is what you base your hope ON. It, the Word, is the substance you base your hope on. If you have not yet reached the place that you know that the entire Word of God is true for you, you cannot base your hope on it. You do not yet have faith, because there is no substance; you just have vague hope, a wish for better things.

You have to know and believe God's blueprint, His Word, in order to let it give you the image in your head of what He says is yours before you get it.

You have whatsoever you believe. Whether you believe a lie or the truth, that's what you'll get.

But if you have let your mind become more crowded with

secular books, or T.V. programs, or movies or humanistic psychology, **more** than it is with God's Word, you will have a hard time until you systematically replace those of the old worldly reasonings with God's concrete truths. Faith comes from hearing the Word (Romans 10:17), again and again until the old has been washed away, and the new takes its place.

It may be difficult because doubt has been subtly creeping into the church. Some churches now teach that the mighty examples written about Noah, Adam and Eve, Moses, and Samson are merely fables. When the issue of believing the ENTIRE Bible is considered you will realize that there is no room for the theory that certain portions are applicable and others aren't. That is setting yourself up as God. Either God's Word is always trustable, or He lies sometimes. Romans 3:4 tells us that God never lies. **So read and believe the whole Word of God until it is absolutely YOURS, and then you will have what you believe.**

Roadblock Number Eight

Having *a passive faith* is also a hindrance to receiving from the Holy Spirit, and is our EIGHTH ROADBLOCK.

The battle in which the Christian is engaged is not one to be approached passively, but AGGRESSIVELY! Passivity in the heat of battle is deadly! This is not a battle of flesh and blood, but against evil principalities and powers, the rulers of darkness. It cannot be won without daily being conscious of what you're thinking, how you are speaking, how you are praying. An example of a passive prayer is one that ends with "if it be Thy will, oh God." That statement takes all the authority out of your prayer. **How much better to know the will of God** *(His Word is His Will)*, and pray His will. If you are very familiar with the character of God you will know what you can expect from Him. You will then pray the aggressive prayer of faith.

Some people argue that Jesus prayed "Thy will be done" in Gethsemane. Let's look closely at it.

"Oh my Father, if it be possible, let this cup pass from me; nevertheless not as I will but as Thou wilt"
Matthew 26:39

He *KNEW* the Father's will was for Him to die on that cross because He and the Father had planned for Him to be the *"lamb that was slain from the foundation of the earth"* (Revelation 13:8). They had formed the world together and agreed on the plan of redemption together way back before Creation. In other words, Jesus was saying, "I sure don't feel like it now, but go ahead with the plan, my Father." It is not wrong to tell God our feelings, but we must know His will and pray IT. Just like Jesus.

His will for Jesus was victory over Satan. His will for us is victory over Satan.

We cannot do that passively. We must know Jesus, constantly watch His example in the Word as to how He dealt with the enemy, and do exactly the same.

Roadblock Number Nine

The NINTH ROADBLOCK is letting your upbringing get in the way of your character.

Too often I hear people say, "Well, I'm negative because my parents were, so I can't help the way I am." Or, "I was the middle child, so I got cheated." Or, "I'm the youngest so I was spoiled by my parents." He is not limited as your parents were. He is the best Parent in the world. He made you for Himself, not for your earthly parents. In fact, the Word says that *"those who come to God must believe that He is, and that He is a rewarder of those who diligently seek Him"* (Hebrews 11:6). HE knows how to bring about the supernatural transformation in your life. **You have His WORD on it.** How?

You can overcome this problem **if** you diligently study God's Word, and get to know His character. It's only your mind which has been badly programmed, and it can be re-programmed. *"Be ye transformed by the renewing of your mind,"* (Romans 12:2) is a command that God would not have given us unless we were able to DO it. **Little by little He will make you a new creation in your character, as you let His Word replace your old mind-sets that keep you tied to old pattern habits.** He will not mess up any talents or personality traits that He has given you from birth. He will only change what has been molded by the world since your birth that NEEDS changing. Nor will you be molded into someone else's character. You will stay uniquely your own person, as He intended.

> *"Let this MIND be in you which was also in Christ Jesus, who , being in the form of God ...took upon him the form of a servant, and was made in the likeness of men."*
> Philippians 2:5

This was Jesus, God in the flesh, taking on the character of man (in flesh and in His MIND) to communicate with us. We do the same thing going in the other direction. We are flesh, taking on the character of God (in our spirit and in our MINDS) to communicate with Him.

Roadblock Number Ten

The TENTH ROADBLOCK is that sneaky, often hidden problem called SELF-CONDEMNATION. This one often starts from childhood as well. If you simply could never do enough to please your elders, you may be tempted to believe that you will not be good enough to please God. You may think that you will not receive the good things you read in His word, even though the Bible tells you differently.

The good news is that you *will never be good enough to receive from God. Never!* Get that settled in your head. None of us is ever good enough, ever!

You receive from God just because **He is a GIVER.** It is He who wants you to have the best because you are HIS. The Word says,

"Eye has not seen nor has ear heard, nor has it even entered into the heart of men the things that God has prepared for those who love Him."

I Corinthians 2:9

According to this you cannot even imagine in your wildest, most wonderful dreams the great things that God has planned for you **that you will never deserve. You love Him, and He loves you.** He gives you the opportunity to hear the Word and believe it, and operate in the fullness of the Spirit, as you TAKE that opportunity. **You have what you TAKE** of what you believe He has given.

A key to receiving "things God has prepared" for me is to love those He sends my way. This is where I apply the statement that faith without works is dead. If I claim to have faith, but do not do the works of God, my faith is immature.

Consider the example of Barnabus and Paul, who had traveled on their missionary journey to the Island of Paphos. When they arrived at their destination, they met the County Deputy, Sergius Paulus, and a sorcerer, a false prophet named Barjesus. Barjesus tried to thwart Barnabus and Paul's attempts to convert the Deputy who had requested to hear the Word of God. Paul, however, was filled with the power of the Holy Ghost and asked Barjesus why he was trying to pervert the ways of the Lord. Paul even called him a child of the devil! Then he said,

"'And now behold, the hand of the Lord is upon thee; and thou shalt be blind, not seeing the sun for a season.' And immediately there fell on him a mist and a darkness, and he went about seeking someone to lead him by the hand."

Acts 13:11

The result of that supernatural power of the Holy Ghost was the conversion of Deputy Sergius Paulus.

The *roadblocks to walking in the fullness of the Spirit* were not keeping Paul from ministering. He refused to be intimidated by FEAR of men in high places (the deputy), or the FEAR of men in the occult (Barjesus). He had loved and revered the Jewish Holy Scriptures all his life, both before and after His conversion to Christ, his Messiah, and was oblivious to anything else the world had to offer. After He saw that Jesus was the one He had been reading about all his life in the Hebrew prophecies about the coming Messiah, he became totally zealous for the Lord Jesus. The Scriptures had so renewed His mind that he wanted nothing less.

We can do the same. We have everything Paul had. Even more, since we now also have what HE wrote! Don't wait around for someone else to give you a good example, if there are only powerless people around you. It is YOU He is dealing with! Will YOU be the one who **hears and obeys even though most of the present day lukewarm Laodicean church is not?** (Revelation 3:16) **Will YOU?**

Let's look at someone who had a successful ministry: **JESUS. Jesus** had no buildings. **Jesus** had no large, committed congregation. In fact, He lost His entire congregation in one day when He spoke to them of their eating His flesh and drinking His blood. They said, "This is too much!" and the whole church left. Only the twelve disciples told Him that they didn't have any place else to go so they stayed with Him.

Jesus didn't have an expensive home. In fact, He said that foxes had holes and the birds had nests, but that He had no place to lay His head. Obviously, His success was not to be measured by today's standards.

Success to Jesus was in fulfilling the vision He had for His Church. He was successful as He set the captives free, healed the sick, preached deliverance and opened the eyes of the blind.

Is your church going about the business of doing the works of God? Is it preparing the bride of Christ? Is it removing the bondages and setting the members of the congregations free? **Look out for the Roadblocks, don't let them stop you, and keep on going!**

Chapter Seven
The Forgotten Ministry: Discerning of Spirits
(I Corinthians 12:10)

The subject of spirits (often called "demons" by Jesus) may be entirely new to you since it is not often preached in most churches. Sometimes it is talked about in a very general manner without ever being fully expounded on. Churches teach that Christians are involved in spiritual warfare, but don't go much farther, and are generally fearful of touching that area. They shouldn't be! Twelve of those references to "spirits" were taught by Jesus Himself. Do we want to be like Jesus in EVERY way? Yes, Church, let's DO IT!

When we are walking in the fullness of the Spirit **any diligent believer** can learn from the Word of God and the Holy Spirit how to discern evil spirits and get rid of them as Jesus did. The word "spirits" is mentioned 20 times in the New Testament in connection with words like "unclean", "wicked" and "evil."

Those who deny the existence of demons are hurting themselves and protecting the hiding demons. It is their tactic to hide. It is guerrilla-warfare, convincing the victim that the enemy isn't really there. The enemy's biggest weapon is deception. If he can convince you that the problem you have is just your personality or some natural cause, he can keep harassing you undetected. If you *discern the spirits* for what they really are, you can have victory over them. It is time to remove the blinders placed over the eyes of the church by the devil.

What are demons? Where did they come from? The twenty times the word "spirits" occur, as mentioned before, is only a part of the one hundred and forty-four times that demons are referred to in the New Testament. Jesus spent more time casting out demons than He did teaching about salvation! Is that ratio happening in your church?

Salvation must never be minimized—it is the first and foremost cornerstone of our faith. We must teach it first, because without Jesus' forgiveness of sins there is no conquering over the enemy. But just teaching salvation without going on to the discerning of the spirits (which torment us or our loved ones) keeps the church looking weak and helpless. When the tormented come for help and we have no answers, what does that say to a hurting world? Jesus never turned the hurting demoniacs away.

Psychics teach that spirits are the departed spirits of the dead who simply didn't make it to either heaven or hell. They are in limbo, floating around for eternity. Some religions believe that they are dead people coming back from death to visit or harass.

There is no place in the Bible where spirits are described as floating around. Instead, the Bible teaches that when we die our spirits either go to heaven or hell.

The Bible, our ultimate authority, also tells us that demon spirits are fallen angels. In the beginning, Satan (then called "Lucifer," meaning "Enlightened") was a beautiful angel in Heaven. He rebelled against the Lord, and God put him out of heaven, casting him into the earth. At that time a great multitude of angels went with him: **they are the demons.**

" How art thou fallen from heaven, O Lucifer, sun of the morning, how art thou cut down to the ground which did weaken the nations, for thou hast said in thy heart, 'I will ascend into heaven, I will exalt my throne above the stars of God, I will sit also upon the mount of the congregation

in the sides of the north, I will ascend above the heights of the clouds. I will be like the Most High,'

Yet thou shalt be brought down to hell to the sides of the pit, that they who see thee shall narrowly look upon thee and consider thee, saying, 'Is THIS the one that made the earth to tremble? that did shake the kingdoms? that made the world as a wilderness and destroyed the cities thereof? that opened not the house of his prisoners?'"

Isaiah 14:12-17

When Isaiah said that he "opened not the house of his prisoners," he referred to the fact that when Satan gets someone in his control, he never **voluntarily** lets them go. This is why discerning of spirits is so desperately needed in the churches. Those demons must be forced out, cast out of the people enslaved by them, because they will never voluntarily leave.

Medical science has nothing to deliver people from demon spirits. Shock treatments given in some institutions, drugs and psychiatry are all ineffective against demons. The only thing that will drive out a demon is the power and authority of Jesus. This is what He was referring to when He said He came to set the captives free in Luke 4.

When Satan was ejected from Heaven, his followers went with him. Peter told us that,

"God spared not the angels that sinned but cast them down to hell and delivered them into the chains of darkness to be reserved into judgment."

II Peter 2:4

Revelation 12:9 says,

"And the great dragon, which deceiveth the whole world, he was cast out into the earth, and his angels were cast out with him. "

Satan and his demons appear frequently in the Old Testament. There was the evil spirit who spoke to God IN HEAVEN and said he would be a lying spirit in the mouth of Ahab's prophets. And so God gave him permission to go to those four hundred and fifty prophets and deceive wicked King Ahab (I Kings 2:22).

The story of Job is another example of Satan's influence. He appeared before God and asked permission to tempt Job (Job 2:1-7). His purpose, after all, is to try to destroy God's people in order to get even with God. Jesus said Satan's mission in life is to "steal, kill, and destroy" (John 10:10).

But Satan is not omnipotent, and cannot be everywhere at once as God can. Satan is only a fallen angel. Satan can only be where he presently IS. He sends his demons to do his bidding unless there is important business to handle. That explains why it was Satan himself who was involved in the temptation of Jesus in the wilderness (Matthew 4:1-12). He also entered Judas Iscariot (Luke 22:3), and he will be embodied in the man of sin, the false prophet, at the end of the world (II Thessalonians 2, Daniel 5:2, Revelation 13:1-14).

Most of us are not a big enough threat to the enemy to have him deal with us himself, personally, on a one-to-one basis. Our problems come from his lesser spirits that have been appointed in his hierarchy over different sections of each country. Ephesians 6:12 speaks of different levels of authority i.e., *"principalities," "powers," "rulers,"* etc. Daniel spoke of a magnificent godly angel who said it couldn't get through to help him any sooner because an evil spirit kept him away,

"the prince of the kingdom of Persia withstood me

twenty-one days: but lo, Michael, one of the chief princes, came to help me"

Daniel 10:13

We must not begin commanding Satan around. Even angels did not personally command Satan (Jude 9). Since we do not know where Satan is at any given time, it would be foolish of us to command him. To do so just shows the spirit-world how little we know, and they don't obey ignorance, only real authority.

This brings me to another subject that may be foreign to you—that of the possibility of Christians having demons. There is considerable controversy among Christians leaders over this.

The popular opinion is that Christians cannot have a problem with demons, and that only unsaved people can have demons. This is false teaching. God never indicated this in His Word. In fact, Jesus sent the Apostles to **deliver His own,** the lost sheep of the house of Israel, the Old Testament equivalent of the church. They were told NOT to take their gifts to the Gentiles and Samaritans, the Old Testament equivalent of the unsaved sinner.

I am concerned that those who teach otherwise are aiding the demons in their quest for safety in hiding, rather than advancing the battle against those "principalities, powers and spiritual wickedness." How sad that **the very people who should be taking the battle to the front lines to defeat the devils are teaching a doctrine that helps the enemy!**

So many Christians tell me they believe that a Christian cannot have a demon because **the very presence of God** in them from the time of their salvation keeps demons out. If that were true, the very presence of Jesus, God in the Flesh, would have kept Satan out of His presence; but even when

Satan was tempting Him (Matthew 3), the Devil hung around and talked with him until Jesus **commanded Him to go, out loud!**

In many instances, demons came **to** Jesus and talked to Him through demoniacs, (Matthew 8:31, Mark 1:34, 5:6, Luke 4:41, Luke 8:30,31) and again, each time, they did not leave His presence until He **commanded them to. Jesus is our example, Church. We must do the same.**

God's presence in you does not repel demons.   Your commands with God's authority *does*. *Just like Jesus,* Church!

Now let's look more carefully at that earlier Old Testament example of demons who were **free to be in God's holy presence** in the story where they were conversing with Him in Heaven. The wicked King Ahab (husband of evil Jezebel) had 450 prophets at Baal, and God told a lying spirit to go and deceive Ahab through his prophets.

> *"And the Lord said, 'Who shall persuade Ahab that he may go up and fall at Ramoth-giliad?'*
> *And there came forth a spirit, and stood before the Lord, and said, 'I will persuade him.'*
> *And the Lord said unto him, 'Wherewith?'*
> *And he said, 'I will go forth, and I will be a lying spirit in the mouth of all his prophets.'*
> *And He said, 'Thou shalt persuade and prevail also; go forth and do so.'"*
> I Kings 22:22-23 and II Chronicles 18:21-22

Also, in the other account in the Book of Job, it said that Satan appeared **in God's very presence** (probably the throne room according to the context of the story) and asked permission to tempt Job.

> *"And again there was a day when the sons of God came*

to present themselves before the Lord, and Satan came
also among them to present himself before the Lord."

Job 2:1

There he is again in God's presence, and he doesn't leave again until **God tells him to.** God allowed Job to be tempted by the Devil to give up. But Job finally heard the truth, saw his pride, and repented (Job 40:4,5; 42:1-6). THEN God restored everything Job had allowed Satan to steal from him.

We cannot let the teachings and traditions of MEN influence our *gift of discernment of demons if we are going to set the captives free!*

"...in vain do they worship me, teaching for doctrines the commandments of MEN"

Mark 7:8

Many who teach that Christians can't have a devil have never delivered any one, Christian or non, so it is just a point of (incorrect) doctrine for them. This makes it safe for demons to hide in God's precious Church. How much it must sadden God that so many of **His** *"people are destroyed for lack of knowledge."* (Hosea 4:6)

Using Jesus' power, I have delivered so many dear Christians who had been bound and driven all their lives by such things as:

* **spirits of jealousy** that divided their families generation after generation

* **spirits of fear** that stifled their wonderful God-given talents

* **harassing spirits** causing chronic severe depression

How I love to watch people enter into the freedom that Christ promised. He wants us to have ALL of His freedom, not just part of it.

We must use our God-given gifts to discern whether these personality disorders are chemical-induced, or learned inappropriate social behavior, or demons. That's what the *gift of discerning of spirits is for, to discern if the spirits are there.* If they are not, we can deal with the problem with other Godly solutions. Our Heavenly Physician wants **us** to have the ability to diagnose spiritual problems, and for this He gave us **Discerning of Spirits.**

Part of the controversy involving Christians and demons stems from our misunderstanding of the word "possessed" (in the Greek meaning "having a demon"). The Bible itself uses the word, and we have taken it to mean that someone is mentally out of control or going wild. This is only if the devil is in someone's mind. The demons can be in any part of the body, the stomach, the feet, etc. The references to possession meant that **the person possessed a devil, NOT that the devil possessed the person.** This refers to demons within someone. Demons outside the person can *oppress or depress.*

There is a popular teaching that there is **a "blood line"** that the devil cannot cross, and therefore, we as Christians cannot be bothered by demons. I have searched the Bible and can find no such thing as a "blood line" mentioned. I believe that anything as important as that would definitely be mentioned, but it is not there. Do not trust in such a teaching because it will not keep you from being bothered by spirits. Conversely, this false doctrine will **protect** the devil from being ruled by YOU! You cannot discern spirits if you already believe their lie that they can't come past a line that isn't there.

The blood of Christ saves us from God's wrath **ONLY.** It saved the people of Israel from **God's** hand of Death on the

First Passover in Egypt. (Exodus 12:29) Only the blood on the doorposts kept the families inside those protected homes from death. Then the high priests were to continually sacrifice animals in the Temple to atone for the sins of the people. **The blood kept the people safe from God's wrath for their sin.**

The blood does not keep us from Satan's wrath. What keeps us from Satan's powers is God's Word. **The Word is our weapon against Satan's forces.** Absorb THE WORD. Speak THE WORD. Learn how to use the Word against the enemy's forces. Command their submission to *the Word. It is the Word of God that is our weapon against Satan (Ephesians 6).*

If this forgotten ministry gift, **Discerning of Spirits** (I Corinthians 12), were in operation in modern-day churches **the way it operated in the lives of Jesus and the apostles,** preachers wouldn't have to wonder **if** Christians can have demons because they would know through this spiritual gift that some Christians have them residing in them.

I know in my own life that there were times when I thought the doctrines of men seemed so absolutely of God, that I argued them with anyone, even though I learned later that they were not Biblical. For instance, I believed that no Christian who smoked could possibly get filled with the Holy Spirit because I had been taught (and thoroughly believed) that since we are the temple of the God, no unclean person such as a smoker would be rewarded by His infilling. The Holy Spirit would refuse to enter.

Later, I was used of God to get a brother gloriously filled with the Holy Spirit, joyfully speaking in tongues. Later I learned that he was a smoker. If I could have, I would have taken the Holy Spirit right back out of him, I was so upset! It was soon afterward that I realized my learned doctrine did not fit in with the Grace of God who **gives** gifts unto men. The Holy Spirit's filling is not a reward, it is a gift of Himself to us so that we may gain the needed power **over** sin. Not the other way around.

Don't let the doctrines of men do the same to your Biblical understanding of demons in Christians. God's presence in you does not deter spirits. The only thing that will make them leave is your **commands for them to leave**, based on your authority in Christ.

Think for a moment about the person who comes forward for salvation after a preacher has presented him with Jesus. Suppose that this person had a demon operating in his life when he went to church that evening. He is offered salvation and accepts Him as his savior, but no effort is made to free him from the demon. Bear in mind that this could be anything from bondage to alcohol, other drugs, fear, etc. **When is the deliverance supposed to take place?** Right... it needs to be done!

Jesus said,

"Now shall the Prince of this world be cast out."

John 12:31

He is to be cast out—not put up with!

HOW DO DEMONS GAIN ACCESS INTO CHRISTIANS?

Remember that spirits are always around, producing irritations that the whole world considers to be part of normal life. They are in every city and every country. They are in the air, and rightly so because it was God Who cast them out of Heaven onto the earth (Isaiah 11). Satan is the Prince of the power of the air.

Satan's presence serves a purpose. We had to have a training ground, the Earth, in which to experience how to rule and reign later, forever with Christ over the whole cosmos. That was part of God's plan from the beginning. God's battle plan was set up and perfect. **If we choose His way, Jesus' way, we win.**

But Satan's cohorts are not gentlemen. They butt in where they are not invited. This is a list of what to be on guard against.

1.) One way demons can come in is through **traumas where you are not in charge of a situation,** for instance, accidents where a head injury is sustained, or a disease that weakens. These are **weakened areas, i.e., "doors"** that the enemy uses to gain entrance. If the armor of God wasn't used properly to protect him, as we are told to do every day (Ephesians 6), a demon can see its chance to find a safe dwelling through those circumstances.

They can be put out easily and immediately. However, the longer they remain, the more entrenched they become, and must be dealt with in stronger terms later.

2.) Christians are open to attack even **when they unintentionally place themselves in situations where they are susceptible, and don't know how to rebuke the enemy immediately** (places where demons have lots of control, i.e., bars, places where drugs are used, homes where evil is prevalent, asylums, etc.). Even though the Christian sometimes dozes on the battlefield, the enemy of his soul does not sleep.

3.) Another way they gain entrance is through a person's **deliberate lack of self control in a weakness where they just obey a temptation and enjoy a sin rampantly, publically OR SECRETLY** (i.e., jealous outrages, lying habitually, sexual perversions, laziness, temper tantrums, manipulation over others to get their own way, etc.). This **weakened area is an open invitation to a demon; a welcome mat.** This is not just daily small temptations that we all have and repent of. This is deliberate sinning against your knowledge of the right way to live for God. Open rebellion is an obvious invitation to a demon. Soon it is no longer your choice, but demons see your open door and enter. **Then they begin to be in control of the habit instead of you.** Before they entered, you were in control. That is oppression from the outside. Now they are in control of **that part** of yourself, and that part only. This is not possession of your whole self, as I explained earlier.

It often **feels like** just a part of your personality, and the enemy lies and tells you it is just you. That is a normal part of their deceit. So many people I have delivered from demons mention the fact that they really were convinced, before their deliverance, that it was just their own thoughts, not the spirits' voices in their minds (see next chapter about how to keep them out once you're delivered).

4.) Constantly fantasizing about sin and failure to control your thinking are open doors. We are commanded to renew our minds. This is why Paul taught the early church,

> *"I BEG you therefore, brothers, by the mercy of God, that you present your bodies, a living sacrifice, holy, acceptable unto God which is your reasonable service. And be not conformed to this world, but be transformed by the renewing of your mind..."*
>
> Romans 12:1-2

This is so important. Especially after deliverance, because unless you **actively work at replacing the old thoughts (i.e. temptations) with the Word, it stays an empty place. A place that has been swept clean of demons is an open invitation for more** (Matthew 12:44, Luke 11:25).

Of course the best way of all to keep from having an open door is to keep your mind renewed every day in the Word as a matter of habit! Keep it washed clean by the daily washing of the Word. Only then does the Word become more normal than sinning again.

5.) Dabbling in witchcraft (no matter how widespread and "innocent" this practice has become) leaves you wide open for trouble with demons, as does practicing Eastern religions. Consulting a psychic is asking the enemy for advice, i.e., witchcraft. A psychic is nothing more than a person allowing a spirit to produce a manifestation of the spirit world. This activity is an avenue that demons travel frequently. What an open door! Stay away from it!

Occult demons require deliverance by another Spirit-filled person. Self deliverance does not work here! This is because you cannot walk away from the occult which is Satan's domain, and expect him to calmly turn you loose without a fight, even though you may have a fantastic experience with God.

Isaiah 14:17 says that Lucifer (Satan) *"opened not the house of his prisoners."* In other words, he does not just let you go. You must get the soldiers of God who know what they're doing to fight, with you, on this one. Take heart, I've seen this battle won many times (see details in Chapter 10).

6.) Ouija boards, viewed by many as toys, are operated by evil spirits or demons. Don't be deceived. I am aware of many cases where demons have manifested themselves through Ouija boards and have continued to torment the persons playing with them for years afterwards. **Horoscopes and fortune tellers are of demonic origin.** How the enemy hopes you will just dabble in these so he can gain a small toehold to start with. Don't read the horoscope in the newspapers. Why subject yourself to the evil spirit-world when it is just as easy to ignore them? Be wise, dear Church.

If you have not already done so as a Christian, you need to go over every inch of your home carefully and prayerfully to find and dispose of anything that would be a foothold for the enemy. Throw away those Ouija boards, any Indian, African or Buddhist idols. You may not consider these statues to be idols, but the devils recognize them for their original intent for their master's kingdom. As far as the enemy's spiritual kingdom is concerned, if you have idols in your house, **they are an invitation to devils** and they know that gives them a right to be in your house, even if you don't know it!

I could give you so many examples of how they get into these articles. It is done on purpose, but kept secret. I learned one from an Indian in Arizona who was bragging one day about the tiny holes drilled into each piece of jewelry which is sold to tourists along the highway. **Those holes were placed there so spirits would have homes in them!** And if you knew the ritual that goes along with the making of each "god's eye," where one extra-long string is always added for a spirit to hang on to, you would throw them all away as well. Don't be deceived. They are not idle coincidences.

I am reminded of people who proudly proclaim to be good, "white witches." Witches are witches. Satan can deceive anyone with good looking prosperity for his sake as well as evil looking manifestations. Some of these dear people caught up in the witches' world don't even know where their power is coming from (although many do when they get deeper into it, but they don't want you to know until you're hooked). When our Heavenly Father is not the one asked, an alternate spirit will gladly answer. **We are commanded to have nothing at all to do with them (Deuteronomy 18:10-12).**

7.) The area of drugs is another place where Christians can be fooled. Unlawful drugs and drug abuse put Christians in deep enemy territory. Drugs are mind-controlling. When someone is not in full control of their mind, this is a weakened area and demons find that open door. The drug scene from the 60's and 70's was a gift to humanity from the Devil. The new masses of zombie-like, brain-burned people in the metropolises are such a testimony of proof that the enemy really wants humanity hurting and dead! How could we have been so duped into thinking that partying would ease our stressful lives?!

Alcohol is a drug, and the same things apply. It is a mind-controlling substance. Who do you want in control of your mind? **I know Christians who use the admonition to Timothy from his spiritual father, Paul,** *"Use a little wine for your stomach"* **(I Timothy 5:23) as an excuse to drink alcohol.** Nonsense! The tiny amount of alcohol in the wine of those days nowhere reaches the content in the wines of today; as well as the fact that the little amount helpful to your stomach would not even get you high! The Scriptures are clear:

"Do not get drunk with wine."

Ephesians 5:18

"They drink the wine of violence."

Proverbs 4:17

"Wine is a mocker, strong drink a brawler."

Proverbs 20:1

"envyings, murders, drunkenness, revelings"

Galatians 5:12

It didn't take any national surveys or surgeon general for God to warn us that wine is closely associated with abnormal behavior and violence! He had said it for thousands of years! He knew how weaknesses allow in demons, and wanted us not to be deceived. Oh, how He loved us all along! If we had only listened!

8.) Depression is another areas that causes such weaknesses that demons may enter. Included in this area is self-pity and discouragement. These all need to be fought off before they increase to the point where possession is eminent.

All demons are not the same. The hierarchy in the spirit world produces demons of different strengths, as well as different characteristics. There are strong demons that cause suicide and murders and some diseases. There are other lesser demons that cause other sicknesses and pain. Often, the pain from these lesser demons may have no real medical basis. You deliver the person from the symptom (pain) and there is no sickness!

Some demons produce multiple personalities, as covered in the book and movie, *The Three Faces of Eve*. The story was a factual one that psychologists have documented. I have seen and delivered many of these. As in the case of Eve, there were several different demons within her. Periodically one would take control and produce a different character. This is not uncommon.

Another famous example of demon possession was a seventeen year old woman in the Philippines named Clarita Villaneuva. She was in a prison cell in the middle of a room so situated that she could be seen clearly through any of the barred walls. Each day she was attacked by an unseen force that caused her to fight and beat the air, scream and kick. When she was examined after these attacks, the authorities found that she had wet bite marks on her arms, black hairs under her fingernails, and other unexplainable evidences of an actual fight. Even the hairs were analyzed and could not be identified as any type that was known to exist on earth.

Word of these attacks filtered out of the prison, and the

story of the "crazy girl" attracted national, then worldwide attention. A book was written about the incidents and the "fights" were viewed by the governor of that area, the mayor of the city, the bishops of the church, and others. Lester Sumrall, an evangelist, happened to be in the Philippines at that time and was asked to see her. He had never been called upon for deliverance before, but nevertheless, he agreed to see her. He went to the prison, took authority over the demons, and cast them out. The demons resisted, but they finally left. **Clarita Villanueva became a normal person and the attacks ceased. This deliverance made national headlines.**

I have seen numerous instances of this as well, and watched people delivered when they **did as I told them.** Seldom do I find just one demon in a person. There are most always two, and the numbers can increase incredibly, as in the case of the demoniac of Gadarah, who had a legion (means "full regiment") of demons in him that Jesus cast out (Luke 8:26-40).

One case of multiple spirits involved a friend's sister who **had been diagnosed as a psychotic for seven years.** She had psychiatric care, received shock treatments in the state mental hospital, had been given drugs, and had joined different religions, all to no avail. I suggested to my friend that his sister probably had spirits, and he asked me to see her. I met with her and explained what I felt was the problem. I told her it was futile to deliver her if she remained unsaved because Jesus had warned that an empty, unclean house invites more demons (as explained earlier with Scriptures). With much hesitation, she finally agreed to accept the salvation Jesus offers, and asked Him to come in and be the Lord of her life.

I told her to come to church that night, and I would deliver her from those demons. **At that point she was saved but not delivered.** (I like the people in my church to see deliverances so that it becomes very real to them how the enemy works, and how strong Jesus' Holy Spirit is on our behalf! It's not necessary for this to happen in church, but its atmosphere is very conducive to making spirits leave.) Those evil spirits were still in her because salvation alone did not remove them from her. **Only a direct command in the authority and character of Jesus does it.**

That night in church, we cast three spirits out of her. She became a totally normal person from that time forward. The change in her was so dramatic that **thirty-six members of her family were saved when they saw the remarkable change.**

This story is so significant because it draws out the important fact that salvation did not get her delivered from demons. Jesus came into her heart, **but the demons didn't leave her until they were specifically cast out of her.** A great many people get saved with spirits in them, and the church has been remiss in not delivering them immediately afterwards. No wonder so many get discouraged and condemned, and then backslide! They find Christianity too difficult to maintain because they believe some of their ugliest personality traits are themselves, and don't know they are battling spirits.

We must always remember not to go hunting for "a demon under every bush," since many ungodly personality traits just have to be worked out through a personal relationship with the Lord, and obedience to Him. But this does not leave out our responsibility to ask for the gift of discerning of spirits for those who need it so desperately in this evil filled end-times, where so many people have been weakened by drugs, the occult, and blatantly accepted, hurting, immoral lifestyles.

In Psalms 81, verse 8, God says *to His people,*

" Hear, oh My people, and I will testify unto thee; Oh Israel, if thou wilt harken unto me, there shall no strange god be IN thee, neither shall you worship any strange

god."

Satan is a strange god, and so are his spirits. This verse indicates, then, that they could be in me if I, one of His people, don't listen to ("harken unto") Him.

The Apostle Paul warned his church, and therefore us too, *"For if he that cometh preaches another Jesus, whom we have not preached, or if you receive another spirit which ye have not received, or another gospel which ye have not accepted, ye might well bear with him."*

II Corinthians 11:4

"Bear" here is translated, (Strong's Exhaustive Concordance, Greek, #430) "hold oneself up against." **Stand up against any doctrine that denies the existence of demons in people, Christian or non.**

Let's protect the people, not the spirits!

The teaching that Christians cannot have demons is based, I believe, on a misunderstanding of the three elements of a person—the body, the soul and the spirit. They say that it is impossible for a demon and the Holy Spirit to dwell in the same temple. But consider this: *"the temple"* referred to many times in the Bible (First Corinthians 3:16-17, 6:19, John 2:21, etc.) is our **spirit**, the temple of God, *not our flesh.* Demons are in the flesh.

Think of yourself as a small house. In it there are three rooms: a kitchen, a living room and a bedroom. The kitchen is not the living room, nor is the bedroom a kitchen. They all serve different purposes, but together they are one home. Any ONE of them is not a house.

In the same way, one room of our body deals with the spirit, one with the soul, and one with the outer flesh. The three go together to make up one person, but they are separate and distinct. Without any one of the three there is no whole person.

God intentionally showed us this picture when He had His people build the Old Testament temple in the style of man. It had an outer court, an inner court, and the Holy of Holies. The High Priest met God in the Holy of Holies where the Ark of the Covenant was located. This was a secluded inner room within the same building where the animals were sold, sacrifices were taking place, and all sorts of activities and confusion were taking place. **Only the inner area, the Holy of Holies, was in perfect order.**

Now, relating that description to our bodies, salvation (i.e., "meeting with God") does not take place in our flesh. If that were the case, our flesh would be saved from sicknesses, aging, and death immediately. But we know it is still subject to all those infirmities. The soul portion of man is the part housing our emotions, and mind and will, i.e., the connecting link which chooses between obeying the outer body or obeying our inner spirit. The Holy Spirit and Jesus **don't dwell in our flesh, they dwell in our spirit.** The spirit is a distinctly separate part inside our bodies, just as the Holy of Holies is separate from the outer court of the Old Temple.

As you are grasping this principle, you will understand why you can have the Spirit of God **in your spirit** once you have been born again, and still have a demon **harassing your flesh.**

You have heard that,

"Therefore, if any man be in Christ, he is a new creature: old things are passed away, behold all things are become new."

II Corinthians 5:17

The "he" refers to your inner man, your spirit. You **are** a spirit: you **have** a soul, and you **live inside** a body. This verse does not apply to your flesh. If it did, upon salvation, wrinkles would disappear, bald heads would have hair, false teeth would be replaced by real teeth, and sagging muscles would firm up tight. The flesh, where demons can dwell, remains unchanged at salvation. Salvation takes place in your human **spirit** which is totally filled with His Spirit. After salvation, all things look different to you as you begin to live life with His presence within you. Paul tells us that his "inward man delights in the law of God." That's his spirit. But, in his "members is the law of sin." Members means the flesh of his body (Romans 7:22,23).

The current doctrinal position of most denominational churches that **"a Christian cannot have a demon" is totally unfounded in Scripture.** I have talked with dozens of pastors who cannot substantiate this theory with any Scripture, although they still insist on believing it.

Think about this. **The presence of Christ Himself didn't automatically keep Satan away from Him in the wilderness (Matthew 4:1-11).** In fact the Devil stayed and argued with Him until Jesus finally COMMANDED him to go. **Nor did God's own powerful, awesome presence in the throne room in Heaven keep Satan from staying and arguing with God** about the righteousness of Job. He had to be *commanded to leave* (Job 2). So the presence of God within a born again believer's spirit does not automatically keep demons from being within his or her body until they are *commanded to leave.*

And, to finish, let's look at what Jesus said to a non-believer who begged Him for deliverance for her daughter. He almost didn't deliver her because, as he told His disciple when he didn't answer her pleas,

"'I am not sent but unto the lost sheep of the House of

> *Israel.' Then she came and worshipped him, saying, 'Lord, help me!' But He answered and said, 'It is not meet to take the children's bread and cast it unto dogs.' And she said, 'True, Lord, but even the dogs eat of the crumbs which fall from their master's table.' Then Jesus answered and said unto her, 'Oh woman, great is thy faith, be it done for you even as you wish.' And her daughter was made whole from that very hour."*
>
> Matthew 15:23-28

She came for her daughter's deliverance from demons, but Jesus told her that **deliverance was the children's bread,** meaning just for Believers. I've heard it taught that she just wanted healing for her daughter, but it is very clear that she said, *"My daughter is grievously vexed with a devil"* (vs.22). The word "vexed" in Greek means "to be possessed with," and the same story in the Book of Mark says she was *"a certain woman, whose young daughter had an unclean spirit"*(7:25). So he got her delivered, but prefaced it with the statement that deliverance was intended for the Children of God FIRST.

If you need any proof that Jesus meant to cast out devils from His Father's children, there it is. He didn't mean to cast them **only** out of the unsaved. Jesus said to cast them out of the Children because THEY needed to be delivered too.

Oh, how many precious believers are **tormented with condemnation** over something in their lives which they hate, but cannot get rid of because they are told that inner evil spirits cannot be the problem. What a safe place for demons to hide, inside trusting saints protected by false church doctrine! **I have cast out demons from hundreds of believers who were so grateful to discover that the harmful personality trait they thought was them, had been a stupid harassing demon all along!** Let's be serious about reading the Word, dear Church, and grow up once more into a mature POWERFUL Bride to match our Bridegroom in taking a mature stand against these wiles of the devil!

Casting out demons should no longer be an unfamiliar scary subject. The spiritual warfare involved in fighting them off are not carnal but MIGHTY. Why should we be afraid?

"For the weapons of our warfare are not carnal, but mighty to the pulling down of strongholds. Casting down **imaginations***, and every high thing that exalteth itself* **against the knowledge of God***, and bringing into captivity every thought to the* **obedience** *of Christ."*

II Corinthians 10:4-5

Oh, Church, see yourselves walking in **obedience** to Christ's commands to *cast out demons*. Don't believe the thoughts that are **against the knowledge** of the Word of God. Don't listen to whatever else our **imaginations** tell us about demons .

We have now covered the origins and purposes of demons. We have also learned the Biblical principles we need to know about their strongholds and about our much more powerful weapons over them. It is time for me to share some of my experiences and what I have learned about how to deal with demons.

Chapter Eight
Dealing With Demons

Once you have been convinced of the existence of demons, the next step **God will give you is opportunities to deal with them.**

God doesn't give us knowledge just so we can be smart. He wants us **to experience His power** over the enemy to *"prove Himself strong on behalf of them whose heart is perfect toward Him"*(II Chronicles 16:9). A training ground is a place of experience **in warfare**, not just book knowledge.

Our bodies are major areas subject to attack from demons when we have **weak spots** they can seek to enter through. Many people are strong enough to keep them out, both physically and emotionally.

But others have received them, and cannot be healed until the spirit producing their particular illness (physical or emotional) is removed from their bodies. Imagine trying to heal an infection in your hand caused by a sliver without first removing the sliver. It may appear healed on the surface, but eventually it will erupt again until **the source** of the problem is removed. The same thing applies to evil spirits causing sickness. **Remove the demon and the healing can follow.**

Jesus dealt with a *"woman with a spirit of infirmity"* which she had had for eighteen years (Luke 13:11). I liken that condition to present-day arthritis. By the time the woman found Jesus, she was doubled over from this condition. Jesus **commanded** the spirit of infirmity to leave her, and she was immediately able to straighten up and function normally. He did not say, "Be healed," as he did with people who were just sick. Medical help could not do any more than temporarily relieve her arthritic pain because the problem was being **caused by a spirit**, and only the Spirit of God can get rid of an evil spirit!

In another case, Jesus referred to someone as having a dumb spirit.

> *"And one of the multitude said, 'Master, I have brought unto thee my son, who has **a dumb spirit**; and when **he** (the spirit) takes him over, he teareth him; and he foams and gnashes his teeth, and he shrivels away.'"*
> Mark 9:17,18

The boy could not talk. Medical science could not have cured that one, but when Jesus **rebuked** the dumb spirit **out loud the child was able to talk.** There were also blind spirits who kept others from seeing (Matthew 12:22). This does not mean all mute or blind people have spirits! The Gift of Discerning of Spirits must be used to determine whether spirits are present, or if it is just a physical condition.

To people who haven't studied spirits, talk of demons might seem frightening, but spirits are actually **very common.** My belief is that a great many Christians have a problem with some type of evil spirit and genuinely need help just like the people who came to Jesus for help.

I once knew a registered nurse whose attitude toward others was one of genuine love and concern. She was involved in an automobile accident and hit her head on the windshield with such force that the windshield cracked, leaving a small cut on her scalp. She later confided in me that since then she felt there was something wrong with her. She was upset because she simply didn't like people any more.

I suggested to her that she might have picked up a demon in that accident which was causing her change in personality. As I talked with her, the demon spoke through her (not an unusual happening) and informed me that I couldn't remove it! When I commanded it to leave anyway, she was back to her original personality, loving and concerned for others as she had been before. The woman wanted the demon to leave her, but the demon didn't want to go. Remember to **command the demon, not the person.** Discern which is speaking to you during deliverance.

It would have been tragic for this dear Christian lady to have gone through the rest of her life with such an abrupt change in her attitude toward people. Only the **power** of God could change her. Just **trying to love** people again in obedience to the Lord would not have helped her. If she had regularly attended church where there was no wisdom about **spirits in Christians, or discerning of spirits**, she would not have been able to return to ministering love and compassion to a hurting world that needed her.

On another occasion, I talked with a young wife and mother who was being tormented by **a jealous spirit.** She explained that she knew that her husband was faithful. However, each time he left the house for work, she would become uncontrollably jealous, imagining all sorts of things he might be doing or thinking. As I talked with her, I found that she had several spirits within her. When she believed me, and consented to deliverance, they were removed and the jealousy was completely gone.

Characteristics such as jealousies, fears, tempers, depressions and normally related problems can be operating in a person who is **just immature in handling those areas**, and not be demons at all.

However, when they begin to control and ruin one's life,

and these **symptoms are uncontrollable,** and begin to run and ruin one's life, despite Godly counseling and daily nurturing in the Word, they are spirits. Here the Church must develop Her power in the Lord to redeem the people from the enemy's control.

The Gifts and weapons must no longer be left sitting on an ecclesiastical shelf where they are ineffective—as the devils smile!

A young married man complained to me of an **uncontrollable temper** that he saw was destroying his marriage and his relationship with his teenage children. Through Word of Knowledge, I was able to tell him what had happened in his early life that had caused this condition: he had been thrown off a horse, which had then kicked him in the head. At that time a demon had entered. I removed the demon and the problem was solved.

These have been examples of **minor problems that demons cause.** Of course they did not seem minor to the people they harassed and life was very difficult for those Christians. But I want to emphasize how common these things are that too often, we just accept as tolerable personality problems.

What they really are are opportunities for us to obey the Lord as we *"have dominion over"* (i.e., "rule over"), and *"subdue"* (i.e., "put into submission under you") the world around us.

This was God's original command to man from the very beginning in Genesis 1:27,28. Read it again with new eyes, Church! We are to rule over *"every creeping thing that creepeth upon the earth."*

The more I was involved in the deliverance of so many people, the more I became aware of how consistently (in fact it seems like always) **head injuries allow demons in.** According to a teaching disciple of Peter Hurkos (one of the most famous psychics today who are aiding police in solving crimes), Peter had absolutely no psychic abilities until he fell off his roof, landing on his head. A student, in the same class where I heard this, asked whether a chiropractor could adjust her neck to give **her** the same abilities Peter had gotten. She thought the source of Hurkos's power was physical. She didn't recognize the work of evil spirits. **Oh, how dangerously naive we can be to play with such powers!**

Pastor Hammond, a Southern Baptist minister, wrote one of the few good books written about the workings of the deliverance ministry, *Pigs In the Parlor,* (Impact Books, Inc.), a bestseller in the Christian world in the early 1970's. His experiences led him to explain how some **spirits are commonly tied to others.** For instance, under the larger demon of pride, come ego, vanity, self-righteousness, haughtiness, self-importance and arrogance. Although I don't totally agree with the one chapter on schizophrenia, I do recommend the book as informative on the subject of demons.

Demons are not relegated to any particular group of individuals, and no age or class is exempt. In the Bible, and through my experiences, **demons can affect anyone, educated or uneducated, intelligent or simple-minded.** I have delivered policemen, nurses, pastors, and teachers. The list goes on and on. Don't be fooled by status or upbringing, just ask for and depend upon the Gift of Discernment.

Many teenagers who aren't protected by wise disciplining and healthy home environments are especially susceptible to demons because of their association with drugs, rebellion and rock music. I am sure you are aware of the controversy surrounding rock music. The **powerful beat** leaves our systems so **mentally and emotionally weakened** that it opens the door to demons. The accompanying intentional messages to ridicule and rebel against the authority figures (which are there to protect them) also **create more weak spots** where demons may enter. We have already discussed drug problems. It amazes me **how often the very same parents of teens who say that hard rock is just a normal part of a teen's life are the same ones** who later ask for help with their kids on drugs.

Keep your eyes open, Parents! The National Education Association recently conducted a study of 5,000 teen suicides, and found that a **significant number of them were connected with hard rock music.** If you read the details of the Charles Manson case you will remember that after he and a band of his followers had killed and disfigured the pregnant Sharon Tate and her guests in her home, he shouted repeatedly to his followers, "The message is in the music. The message is in the music!" Church, be aware of the avenues the devil uses to subtly destroy our children, and be firm with them about not wandering into his territory. Tough love in this area will pay off in the future even though they will be told by their worldly peers that you just don't understand.

Agoraphobia, the fear of leaving home, is on the increase. Even people who are ordinarily extroverts can fall prey to this problem. I delivered one woman, a very sincere Catholic extrovert from a prominent family. She would not go shopping, would not drive her car, would not leave home for any reason, and would not entertain anyone in her home because she was suddenly afraid of people. She was taken to a large city for treatment in a clinic. After six weeks of trying to determine the cause and find a cure, she was sent home with several bottles of pills. She did not, however, change at all. She still refused to leave the house. I heard of the situation and went to see her. Once she was delivered of the spirit, she returned to normal.

One woman had had monthly **migraine headaches** for twenty years. After talking with her I discovered that she had a spirit in her head. Once it was removed, she too regained her normal health and lifestyle.

One of the worst experiences I ever had was in delivering a woman who had been **playing with back-masking on a record.** When these records or tapes are played backwards an entirely different message is heard. More often than not its message is Satanic in nature. This woman was just **playing** with it, but she got horribly and unreasonably agitated by it and called the church one evening, alternately laughing and crying. I went immediately to her house and found violent spirits had taken her over. I demanded the demons to let her go. They did. She was freed of them and stayed totally free.

Once I knew a young woman who had, in her younger days, been **in bondage to drugs.** She eventually gave her life to the Lord and was an active, growing Christian. However, once a month for a 24-hour period, she became a totally different person, without any control over her life. This is an example of dual personalities, as I discussed earlier. In this case, she had **two distinct personalities,** but the second one took over for only one full day out of each month. At the end of the 24-hour period, she didn't know where she had been, what she had been doing, or whether the police were looking for her for having committed crimes, or what! She normally worked in a hospital and would discover that, although she had left in her white uniform, she would return in Levis, with no idea where her uniform was. She couldn't figure out where she got these changes of clothes. This was terribly tormenting and scary to her, and she just knew she had a mental illness (which is soaring to such new heights in America!). So she came to see me and I delivered her of eight spirits. That second personality left her, and from that time on she was perfectly normal.

Demons show themselves in many other ways to destroy our bodies. A friend was pouring concrete and had what appeared to be a serious heart attack. A doctor examined him and gave him no hope of recovery. He was admitted to the hospital where his pulse and blood pressure were taken every two minutes at his doctor's instructions in the intensive care unit. I was called in by the family. Through discerning of spirits I determined that he had **a demon attacking his heart.** I commanded it to remove itself. The attacks subsided and the next day he walked out of the hospital. He was in church the day after that to tell the story. The day after THAT, he completed the concrete job he had started! Some heart attacks are of this type; some are not. Discerning of spirits will tell which is which.

I have found also that some cancers are caused by demonic activity. A Christian nurse in our church had cancer so severely in both breasts that by the time she got over being prudish enough to tell me she had it (almost a year!), both breasts were hardened and the pain had spread up to the glands in her neck and around to her backbone. She had been trying to get rid of it by prayer for healing, instead of deliverance. She told me, "I've been a nurse long enough to know that even if they remove both breasts, I'll still die because it's gone too far." We had her come in and we cast that cancerous spirit out of her. That was nine years ago. She is still cancer-free today, with several medical checkups to verify it.

Develop that gift, Church. We need it so badly for hurting believers, as well as the world. **Let's obey the Lord Jesus and set these people free!**

While it is difficult for Christians to believe that demons exist in America, they readily believe that demons can exist in Africa or South America. Why is this? Think about it. What do remote areas have to do with demons? Nothing! Three times I have been so far into the inland jungles of Africa that I was the only white man they had ever seen. I lived with them in their huts and ministered to them in their churches. But I can say without hesitation that I have seen far more demons in civilized U.S.A. than in Africa. After all, wouldn't demons be assigned to the place where they could do the most harm? Wouldn't that place be where God's church is thriving the most?

I tell you these stories so you will be prepared for anything a demon might try. They are such lying con-artists. But after a while they run out of their limited scare tactics and nothing surprises you. And after a while it even gets boring because they are such wimps around the authority and power of the Lord working through you. But oh, how I love to watch people who have been set free. The joy on their faces, when they feel the difference, is beautiful to see!

But at first, when you are just getting started things are so new, and you will need to know **what to expect.** When a demon spirit is stirred up within a person, several different things may take place.

Watch for **one or more of the many different manifestations** that show when demons leave. Some are designed to cause fear in you. Others are so medically impossible that they might distract you. The idea is to stay in control.

1. When you exercise enough authority, **the person** in whom the demon is residing **may show considerable fear** of your presence. They may not want you to touch them.

2. Sometimes just hearing about demons **will cause demons to react noisily** and interrupt a service.

3. The person who has one (or more) **may feel things moving within their body.** As a rule, people who have demons, and have never been delivered before, do not know they have them. They had just previously thought it was gas or nerves.

During deliverance the demons will often move away from where your hand has been placed on the person, and that really helps the person to realize it isn't just a physical problem.

4. Occasionally, as the demon is getting ready to leave at your command (because he knows from your authority that he HAS to), the person will feel **a fullness in their chest** or **a lump in their throat.** Encourage them to physically expel these. This cooperation of the person with you causes the demon to see that you two are in agreement that the demon **must leave.**

People will sometimes refuse to do this because they do not know that **the demon, hoping it can stay, is causing them to resist.** I have seen people clench their teeth and tightly close their mouths to keep the demons in! I speak to the person here and encourage them not to cooperate with the demon, but to cooperate with me instead.

5. **Yawning often occurs** as smaller demons leave. I have seen people yawn one hundred times or more in a row as the pests came out one by one.

6. Some stronger demons, on the other hand, can come out screaming. **Don't be afraid, this is just to scare you** like an old roaring lion with no teeth! The Word says Satan is *"as a roaring lion"*, NOT *"is a roaring lion"* (I Peter 5:8). He's just an imitator. **It even happened when Jesus was delivering folks** too.

*"And in the synagogue there was a man, which had a spirit of an unclean devil, which **cried out with a loud voice,** 'Let us alone; what have we to do with you, Jesus, son of Nazareth? Have you come to destroy us? I know you, who you are, the Holy One of God.' And Jesus rebuked him, saying, 'Hold your peace and come out of*

him.'

And when the devil had thrown him in the midst he came out of him and hurt him not."

Luke 4:33-35

Did you notice that the unclean spirit was in CHURCH? Don't be surprised to find them in yours. Be ready, be wise, and stay in control!

Did you notice that Jesus didn't argue or reason with the demon? He just commanded it to leave. Be ready, don't argue, and stay in control.

Did you notice that the demon tried another tactic of throwing the man to the ground in the middle of the group? Would that scare you? YOU are the authority! Jesus said *"All authority was given unto Me, therefore YOU go."* Be wise, be calm, be ready, and stay in control.

Because this ministry is relatively unknown and unused in the church (an unfortunate situation) you may be condemned, and even maligned by other Christians as you walk in this Godly gift. You may have more opposition from Christians than you will have from the demons. Sad, but true. **Jesus was also maligned for casting out demons.** And it was the spiritual leaders of the day that attacked Him, too!

"Then was brought unto Him one possessed with a devil, blind and dumb, and He healed him so that he both spoke and saw.

And all the people were amazed, and said, 'Is not this the son of David?'

But when the Pharisees heard it, they said, 'This fellow does not cast out devils, but by Beelzebub, the prince of the devils.'

And Jesus knew their thoughts, and said unto them 'Every kingdom divided against itself is brought to desolation..."'

Matthew 12:22

and then,

"'He that is not with me is against me.'"

Matthew 12:30

When confronted, Jesus taught them the Word, warned them against being divided, and calmly went on doing the same things the Father had told Him to. Healing the sick, raising the dead, casting out demons.

Stay in control of yourself and your emotions, patiently teach them the Word, and don't back down from what the Father has said in the Word to do.

7. **Occasionally a person will gag or vomit** when strong demons leave, but this happens much less frequently than just repeated coughing or yawning.

People unfamiliar with what is going on may watch these lesser reactions and think that nothing has happened. They may not realize that each time the person coughs, he is expelling a demon. **The demons come out one at a time until the strong one is left, and it comes out last.**

Years ago we were taught that if you could name the demons through a Word of Knowledge, the demon would come out easier. Although this is occasionally helpful, it isn't always necessary. **Sometimes Jesus named them, but most of the time He did not.**

The **name of a demon is just the character of that demon,** like "anger" or "infirmity" or "Legion." This naming pattern was established in the Old Testament as God named his saints according to their **character.** "Abraham" meant "father of nations" (Genesis 17:5), Jacob meant "supplanter" but later when Jacob became obedient to God He changes his name to "Israel" (Genesis 32:28), etc. The pattern was, as usual, adopted by Satan and his demons; the old imitator trying to copy and mock God again.

One instance, where **a demon identified itself** in a woman, stands out in my mind. This lady had a beautiful singing voice in total control. She seemed totally normal when I visited her in her home. However, it wasn't long before I discerned that demons were tormenting her. Then I saw her thrown across the room by an unseen force. (No wonder I recall this instance so vividly?)

She told me that at sixteen she had been raped by her father, and subsequently she had been committed to the State Asylum on two separate occasions. She had given up, and, in her tormented condition, had asked Satan to enter her, and he did. When she looked into the mirror, she could mentally see holes in her forehead with snakes crawling in and out of them. **She was truly a tormented captive.** When she was released from the asylum the second time, the staff told her parents that she would be back, and when that happened she would never leave again.

I began to deliver her, commanding each demon to leave. There were several hundred of them. When they were all gone, she was finally set free. The key, dominant spirit was a **spirit of homosexuality.** This spirit talked to me out loud from inside her. Since she was married and had a child, no one ever even suspected she had that problem. She was a Christian, but could not have remained one with that burden of condemnation which Satan constantly used against her in this area.

Homosexuality is a major problem in this country. It **must be dealt with in the spirit**, not with psychiatry. Psychiatry cannot cast out demons. And lately, so many psychiatrists just suggest that it may be an "acceptable alternate lifestyle" anyway. It is NOT! Normal social relationships between men and women have always had to be worked out and are not always easy. **To suggest that the unnatural homosexual relationship between men and men, or women and women, could replace the one created for men and women, is to go totally against Scripture and God's heart.**

Both the Old and New Testaments are very clear on this.

"You shall not lie with a male as one lies with a female; it is an abomination."

Leviticus 18:22

"Professing to be wise, they became fools, ... and therefore God gave them over to the lust of their hearts to impurity, that their bodies might be dishonored among them. ... for this reason God gave them over to degrading passions; for their women exchanged the natural function for that which is unnatural; and in the same way also the men abandoned the natural function of the woman and burned in their desire towards one another, men with men committing indecent acts and receiving in their own persons the due penalty of their error."

Romans 2:22-27

Sounds very clear how God feels about homosexuality, doesn't it? Remember though, that God hates **the sin** because it hurts His creations. He does **not hate the sinner**, and we should do the same.

Let the homosexual know this: he or she is loved by God and can be delivered from what God says is an abomination to Him. This must be dealt with in deliverance from the spirits, even though he or she FEELS like it's just their own personality since birth. No amount of intellectual talk, reasoning, or psychiatry will cure it, once it has begun to drive the person. It is not something one is born with, or a physical problem. It is a problem with **its origin in the spirit realm**, and anyone can be set free if that person wants to be.

Another incident involving **a homosexual spirit** occurred in my church. A young man, who had attended for over six months, admitted that he had been a homosexual (since he was four years old), and realized he needed, and could have, deliverance. Once he came up front to be delivered and he was set free from that spirit (which was in his head, I discovered) **he was totally set free.** You could see it on his face! He was feeling so new. At that point he began to sing a beautiful, **God-given chorus of praise** that was so powerful that it spread all over the country:

> *"Hallelujah, I'm free!*
> *No burden of sin is bothering me.*
> *He paid the price on Calvary's tree.*
> *Hallelujah, I'm free!*
> *Hallelujah, I'm FREE!!"*

That man, and that woman before him, and the millions like them, are the ones to whom Jesus referred when He said He had come to set the captives free.

Once I delivered a young man from **kleptomania.** He loved to steal music records. His parents had to watch him constantly because when he was left unattended, he would sneak into town to steal records. Although he had enough money to buy them, he wouldn't use it. The moment he was found to be missing, his parents drove downtown, trying to beat him to the record store. He was having so many problems that he was permanently expelled from public school. His juvenile probation officer told me that the next time he was caught, he would be placed in the state correctional facility for juveniles, his probation would automatically be revoked, and he would be incarcerated. His uncle and father brought him to me one Saturday morning for deliverance.

He clearly did not want to be delivered! This was the only time I delivered anyone against their will, but he just didn't have any more time for chances to straighten up on his own. There were two spirits in him, and once they were removed the kleptomania tendencies were **gone**. He went back into high school, finished his education, and became a pastor of a large church in our community.

I rarely deliver someone who does not want deliverance because when they leave with the same **rebellion** they came with, **the demons just re-enter them later** through that same weakness, and bring more demons with them just as Scripture says.

> *"Now when the unclean spirit goes out of a man, it passes through waterless places, seeking rest, and does not find it. Then it says, 'I will return to my house from which I came.' And when it comes back, and it finds it unoccupied, swept and in order, then it goes and takes along with it seven other spirits more wicked than itself, and they go in and live there; and the last state of that man becomes worse than the first. That is the way it will also be with this evil generation."*
>
> Matthew 12:44 and Luke 11:25

What a warning! **We must warn those who are about to be delivered** that, once they have been delivered, they need to get saved if they are not; or, if they are Christians they must now stay lovingly obedient to the Lord. Even Jesus, who delivered Mary, said to her, **"Go, and sin no more!"**

In this young man's unusual case I trusted the father and uncle to help him stay free and they did. (See Chapter 9 about how to **keep your deliverance.**)

When you are doing deliverance with others around you, remember that it is YOUR authority *in Christ* that gets the person delivered. **Prayer does not accomplish deliverance. Commands do!** The people around you may pray for strength and wisdom for **you**, others may praise God, but only *one person* handles deliverance at a time.

The person being delivered should not help in any way. They should not pray, or praise or do any activity to "assist" you. This is very important to remember. The person must remain as still and submissive as possible so that when the demon is ready to leave them, it doesn't have to fight to get through the praying or praising. Jesus never asked the person He was delivering to help Him.

Remember again that demons aren't deterred by your prayers anyway. Prayer is communication between you and God. It has nothing to do with your communication with a demon. *Evil spirits only obey your commands backed by your authority in Christ.*

WHERE DO EVIL SPIRITS STAY?

Evil spirits look for **bodies** to live in most of the time. They are not in your spirit unless you are totally POSSESSED, **which they can only do if you gave them conscious permission to have your life** as in the occult. They are found in some area of the physical body (including the head).

The evil spirits are not necessarily in the part of the body where the pain or problem is occurring. Sometimes they show themselves in one area in order to hide from you so you won't get rid of them. They may also give excessive manifestations. In Hollywood's *The Exorcist*, the demon activity was **exaggerated compared to most normal deliverances.** But occasionally those manifestations do take place in someone who has many, many demons, but all those things in that movie will not take place **at the same time** in the same place. You can handle them one by one.

Demons will, however, **attempt** to keep you so busy to try to confuse you. They don't want you to get to the point of taking authority over them. When this happens, **you must order them to stop and to settle down and obey you.** Then they will obey. Don't get excited and don't yell at them. That is just your flesh. Jesus showed calm, strong authority, and so can you. **Stay listening to God.**

Most people have more than just one demon, especially if they have been harassed with a problem over a long period of time. These demons aren't necessarily in the same location in the body. I have found them even in the feet of people, as well as the more commonly found places like the head, the abdomen, the chest and the thighs. **They can be anywhere.**

If, by **the Gift of Discerning of Spirits,** you know where that demon is in the body, and you can discreetly put your hand on it, it will leave there **quicker** than if you just order it to go. Jesus was able to simply order demons to leave, and we can get to that level of maturity as well. However, until you get to that place, it will be easier to remove if you can hold your hand over it, even without touching the person.

I used to wonder why some deliverance sessions took longer than others. **I have found that you sometimes have to deal with the flesh of the person that houses the demons.** People I have delivered have told me that demons had called them by name **in their brains** and told them to help them stay in. Demons get them to clench their teeth or mouth. You must speak to the person and tell them not to believe the voices in their head.

So many times people have told me that **their brains are so unusually quiet after deliverance,** whereas before deliverance, they thought that was just the way a normal brain worked with many voices in it.

Also, I often hear delivered people mention that after deliverance, their **heads feel less pressure,** as in a basketball that has had the extra air pumped out of it to release unwanted pressure. After deliverance let them express these changes to you.

A WORD OF CAUTION

These instructions are not for a novice who has never seen deliverance before. **Demons are not to be played with. You must know that you know *that you know* that you believe that** this power is in you, as Jesus said.

It is important to be wise and remember that you **first find a place** (rare as they may be because of the Church's disobedience in this area) **where you can watch deliverance.** The disciples watched Jesus do this **before** He sent them off to do it. Even then He sent them out at least **two-by-two for agreement and back-up.** And you must do the same. **So, do not attempt deliverance alone.**

The Sons of Sceva (Acts 19:14) really thought they could deliver men from demons, but ended up being beaten by them instead. If they had known Jesus, and gotten under His ministry, and watched Him and heard His instructions, they would not have been beaten. But they went off **without His authority and teaching,** and so they failed.

I am **setting you up for success,** as Jesus did, not for failure. Find out what Jesus said, and do it HIS WAY. Your faith (not someone else's) based on His Word (not someone else's) will never fail.

OTHER MANIFESTATIONS

When you first get involved in this ministry, you may find that the person you are delivering **may fall the minute you touch them.** On occasion a demon will take the person over, knocking them down. The person recedes to the background, and the demon becomes prominent. It may begin talking though the person and showing strength. As you realize the authority you have over these demons these manifestations will stop. They won't try after they have **seen that you have never backed down.**

In the beginning, however, you may find that you have to hold the person to keep him or her from getting violent. (Another good reason to always have someone else present.) **Stay in charge and command them to keep coming out.** They **WILL flee.**

"Resist the devil, and he will flee."

James 4:6

It is God's Word and you can count on it!

There have been, however, extreme reactions **to** demons by men who are **still learning** to deliver in Jesus' Name. The ministers get louder and more violent as the demons do. This is ridiculous! **Jesus never got out of control like that! He strongly and calmly rebuked them** again and again (Matthew 17:18, Mark 9:25, Luke 4:35, 9:42). We must do the same.

"And Jesus rebuked him, saying ,'Hold your peace and come out of him.'"

Mark 1:25

Quite often, the demons will talk, attempting **to intimidate** the person who is casting them out. They may begin **to threaten** the person. Then they might try **to bargain** with the person doing the delivering. If that doesn't work they might try **to plead** with you.

They tried ALL of these on Jesus too. None of these techniques worked with Him (read the four Scriptures cited above). Don't let those tactics work with you either.

When delivering the demoniac of Gadara, demons begged Jesus not to send them into *"the deep."* He sent them into pigs instead, who immediately ran wildly into **the lake** anyway! He never obeyed a demon's request.

In one case a demon said to me, "I have my fingers entwined in her inside-organs and I'll pull them out with me."

I said. "Go ahead," and the intimidated demon replied, "I'll do it later." I told him he had to do it right now. He said, "No, I guess I won't." Then I cast him out, and out he came. If I hadn't **known** that he couldn't accomplish his threats, I **may have been intimidated** and left him alone.

I'm NOT saying you should ever play with them. This event took place before I realized I didn't have to answer them. But I use this example only to show that we are to **stay in control of the demons who would like to intimidate us by manipulating our fears.**

Suicides are a major problem among teenagers and our elderly people. I recently read an article in *The Accelerator* (vol. XXI), a National Christian education magazine, that, *"the poisonous effects of HUMANISM have seen 5,000 U.S. teens commit suicide during the first School Quarter (ALONE!), and another 100,000 tried and failed during the past 12 months."*

I have yet, in twenty-five years, to work with a person with suicidal tendencies who did not have demons in them.

Suicide has become such a national problem that hot-lines have appeared everywhere, offering help. But studies are showing that their success rate is discouraging. No wonder: demons cannot be controlled by psychology.

Suicide becomes a demonic problem when the idea of suicide has been entertained in the brain for some time. In the beginning it feels only like temptations to be discouraged and depressed. These are what the Word refers to as *"fiery darts"* (Ephesians 6:16) i.e., **thoughts from the enemy that we nurse as our own**, not realizing they are lies trying to plant themselves in our brains. But, unfought against, these nursed thoughts of depression, **become** an emotional weakness that unconsciously invite demons to enter and take control. I have a friend who calls these weaknesses "landing pads" or "welcome mats." Those are good analogies of what really happens.

When we **refuse**, by the power of God in us, **to entertain and nurse those thoughts** of depression, self pity, and suicide, we are fighting the good fight of faith (I Timothy 6:12). We must teach people how to recognize when these thoughts enter their heads, so that they can command the demon **outside them** to stop tempting them **from the outside**, before the enemy uses that weakness as a door to enter **in**. (See Chapter Nine on, "Staying Delivered")

In one case, as I was delivering a girl, the demon said, "I am in a great deal of trouble." I asked him, "Trouble with who?" It told me that I already KNEW who! He was right. I knew that in **the hierarchy of demons** (Ephesians 6:12) the demon in authority over him had given him orders to destroy this girl, and he was failing miserably. The demon begged me to give it three more days, and then it would leave. I knew he would be successful in getting her to kill herself by then. Demons do not live in dead bodies. I ordered it to come out, and it did. That was the end of her horrible suicide problems.

Another demon's intended victim was a woman who had attempted suicide eight times. **She came to me from the hospital after the last attempt.** She was delivered and has had no more problems with suicide in the three years since then.

Remember, again, that all sicknesses (i.e., temporary illnesses), diseases (i.e., terminal illnesses), sins, circumstances, personalities, or suicides are *not always demons.* **So always use the Discerning of Spirits before any deliverance.**

DELIVERANCE FROM THE OCCULT

Another fact to remember, when being used of God for deliverance from demons, is that people who have been tied to the OCCULT are handled a little differently in that the occult activities **must be repented of and rejected by the person first.**

If this is not done, the root of the problem, which was a **choice of the heart to serve another god** besides the Lord, will surface again. This is so serious because the sin that God hates the most is idolatry. That is why the first Commandment is *"Thou shalt have no other gods before Me"*(Exodus 20:1).

In the occult involvement a person is consciously serving another god, and remembering the previous Isaiah Scripture, *"Satan never opens the door of his prison,"* he does not **easily** let a person go, especially when they have **chosen** him. He believes you are his forever by your own *confession of allegiance* to him.

Therefore occult-involved people need more help than those who may have picked up demons accidentally. **Lead them,**

    #1.) in recognition and confession of their sin of having chosen another god, and

    #2.) in the repentance and denouncement of their past obedience to the enemy.

This **new** *confession of renouncement* replaces their old *confession of allegiance.* **Then deliver them.**

Many people have believed that they can walk away from their occult experience merely by rejecting it alone and getting saved. However, the fact that they let go of Satan does not mean that he let go of them. They *must always* be **led** through deliverance. **Self-deliverance here is not possible or valid.**

It is not necessary for them to make a list of the activities or things they were involved with that may have resulted in their getting a demon. There is a teaching going around that instructs you to do this, pray over the list, and then get the person with the demon to reject the demon by commanding it to leave as they exhale. This is not Biblical. I once saw a person "delivered" in this way. But the next day I delivered that same person from forty spirits. The job had not been done the day before.

THE STRONGEST DEMONS

The **last demon to leave,** when there are more than one, **is the key demon,** or "strong man" (taken from Matthew 12:29, Mark 3:27, and especially Luke 11:20-21), where Jesus said,

> *"But if I with the finger of God cast out devils, no doubt the kingdom of God is come upon you. When a strong man armed keeps his palace, his goods are in peace; but when one stronger than he* (i.e., Jesus Himself) *shall come upon him, and overcome him, he takes away from him all his armor wherein he trusted, and divides his spoils."*

Only a power stronger than the strongest demon can rule it and tell it where to go. That is the authority of Christ in YOU.

If you do not remove the strongest demon, getting the other little ones will do no good for very long. The rest will simply come back later at the strongman's invitation. You will know by the **discerning of spirits** when this strong one has left. However, if you are not sure of what you are doing, don't try to do it without help and instruction from a more experienced Christian in this area.

When you deal with someone with **hundreds of spirits,** it is best to space the deliverance ministry to them over a two to three day period, **keeping very good track of the person** between deliverances. A believer should stay with them till it is done.

You can also work with the person for a while, then **take a break period before continuing.** It is not necessary to accomplish all the deliverance on the same day, as long as you are thorough, making sure they have all gone once you are completely done.

Remember it is **the quality of your authority in Jesus,** not the quantity. This principle applies in the case of a person with many demons. If you get weary, you can let someone else take over as you stay close by. But even that isn't necessary if you realize you can take as much time as you feel you need.

Stretching out the deliverance process is often easier on the person who needs heavy deliverance. **Deliverance is sometimes painful,** and in your own judgment, you will decide whether you should wait before completing the deliverance.

During one deliverance I noticed the person bleeding from his mouth. He went to be checked by a doctor because he was convinced that I had done something to his throat during the deliverance. I told him that I never touched his throat. His doctor told him. "I don't understand it, but it looks as though someone has reached into your throat and scratched it with their fingernails." **Evidently, when the demon left, it had torn at the throat of the man.**

I shouldn't have been surprised for it's right in the Word. When Jesus delivered a man , the Bible says,

> *"when the unclean spirit had torn him, and cried with a loud voice, he came out of him."*

Mark 1:23

In Luke 9:38-42 there is a story about a man who brought his tormented son to Jesus. This is another case where a demon tore the person. See what Jesus did. He first delivered the child, and then **healed** him before handing him back to his father. We do the same.

Another thing that some people do that is not Scriptural, (which started in the West Coast and spread to the East) is **"mass deliverance."** Jesus didn't do it and we must not either. It only stirs up the demons in people, and some smaller ones may leave, but the **one-to-one ministry is needed for thorough discerning of spirits and their deliverance.** Otherwise, how can you get to the strongman?

Your responsibility does not end with the deliverance. You (or a Mature-in-Christ person from your body of believers whom you have trained, or trust) need to counsel with the person, and attempt to determine how the demon got into them in the first place. You don't deliver them and let them go unarmed against the enemy. Follow-up is as important as deliverance. Those weak areas where the demons entered in the first place must be strengthened to keep them from re-entering.

The next chapter will explain how to do that.

Chapter Nine
Staying Delivered

Remembering back to the instructions of Jesus in Scriptures where He instructs us **what to do AFTER demons have left**, let's review their importance.

> *"When the unclean spirit is gone out of a man, he walks through dry places, seeking rest, and finding none. Then he says, 'I will return into my house from whence I came out;' and when he is come, he finds it empty, swept, and garnished.*
>
> *Then he goes, and takes with himself seven other spirits more wicked than himself, and they enter in and dwell there: and the last state of that man is worse than the first. Even so shall it be also unto this wicked generation"*
>
> Matthew 12:43-45

The Lord must be invited to enter the place where the demons have left, or, as this Scripture shows, it lays empty until some **other spirit** comes into that place.

There is a huge difference between having the demon on **the inside** of you pushing you around, and having an old demon hang around you on **the outside,** tempting you to fear it in the same old ways. Every time you tell it to go away, (i.e., rebuke it) it will get more and more tired of harassing you, and finally hardly ever return. (*"Resist the devil and he will flee from you"* James 4:7) It is a fight, but we can win when we stay wise, obeying the Word.

The delivered person needs to be shown this scripture and reminded of what a serious matter it is to receive deliverance if he does not **intend to** live for the Lord.

If the person is a Christian, they need to ask the Holy Spirit to fill that spot where the demons left with His own Self. Some wisdom on why the demon entered in the first place should be discussed, establishing what can be done to keep the old habits or fears from inviting demons back. The delivered person may not know how they picked up the demon. They may have been born with it; they may have picked it up at a very young age; or they may have picked it up through an experience they have forgotten. Ask the Lord for the Spirit of Counsel (Isaiah 11:2) to help discern this.

One helpful tactic against the wiles of a devil (Ephesians 6:11) is to remind it that you WERE delivered, and it may not come back. By saying aloud something like, "I **was** delivered from you on March 18, 1992 and **you will not** come back in. The Word says when I resist you, you must flee, so GO," you are resisting its re-entry. Remember, James 4:7 says if you resist the devil he WILL flee from you. By this, you establish your personal Biblical right to not be hassled anymore. You can do it again and again and it **will** stop if you stand up to it.

So often when a person has had a demon for a long time, and has adopted the characteristics of that demon (i.e., jealousy, anger, violence, suicide, homosexuality, etc.) it **feels like their own personality.** It has just been there so long that it feels comfortable.

After deliverance you are relieved and notice much less pressure to have these feelings, but they must be **resisted and recognized as a temptation from the outside**, no longer a driven power on the inside. It becomes as you were before the demon entered, i.e., only a temptation, and temptations must be resisted by all believers normally.

I saw a man totally delivered from nicotine for weeks, praising God that he didn't even have the desire for it any more. One day he chose to play with it by smoking to see if it really would stay away, *and he got hooked again!* **You don't play around with God's grace and expect to keep the enemy at bay.** He will use your disloyalty to God to his own evil advantage and then condemn you for it! He is *"the accuser of the brethren"* (Revelation 12:10), and he will accuse you to yourself and others just as readily as you will **let** him by obeying him. It was this man's CHOICE to let the devil return.

So there are certain things a delivered person must never do. They must never get very, very angry, depressed, jealous, or exhibit similar emotional weaknesses. These are the excesses through which the demons came in the first place.

I am not referring to the common, day-to-day emotional highs or lows that we all experience occasionally. I am referring to the extremes which indicate a lack of **control**. Teach the person the **importance of using self-control** (Galatians 5:22), one of the fruit of the Spirit. It comes from spending lots of **time** with Him and renewing your mind in His Word, thereby absorbing His character of self-control.

One more thing you must do as part of the deliverance is to **deliver the person's house as well**, and teach them to do so often. The entire problem the person has had may not be completely dealt with until their home is cleared of any demonic trappings. These physical things have spirit-ties that invite the evil beings into the home. Start by getting rid of the idols that were mentioned in an earlier chapter (ouija boards, god's eyes, foreign figurines, etc.).

Someone once called me to deliver their house, and as I walked through that house for the most part, it appeared to be clear of demons. I came to a solid wood china cabinet, and I knew by the Spirit that behind the doors was a demonic symbol. I told the family that there were demons in that area of the room, and had them open the doors. On the shelf lay a god's eye (a diamond shaped macrame-type of American Indian idol-handicraft). I told them to throw it out in the garbage, which they did. **With that simple act of obedience, most of the problems besetting that house ceased.**

If you feel inadequate to even begin walking in this area of ministry remember Jesus' words:

> *"Verily, verily, I say unto you, he that believes on me, **the works that I do shall he do also**; because I go to my Father, and whatsoever ye shall ask in my name, that will I do, that the Father may be glorified in the Son. If you ask anything in my name, I will do it."*
>
> John 14:12

This is the ability you **have** as a believer. Jesus only qualified the above statement about what YOU could do by saying *as a believer* you could do them. You only need to be a BELIEVER; you do not need to be one of the original Apostles.

Some churches have decided that only the Apostles could do these things and that they were given that ability **only** to get the church established. They may quote the passage from I Corinthians 13:8-10) that says,

> *"Charity never fails; but whether there be prophecies, they shall fail; whether there be tongues, they shall cease; whether there be knowledge, it shall vanish away, for we know in part, and we prophesy in part, but when that which is perfect is come, then that which is in part shall be done away."*

Some would say that this indicates that the supernatural Gifts of Prophecy, Tongues and Knowledge somehow, somewhere vanished! **Where in Scripture did God remove the**

supernatural gifts from the church after He gave them that authority? Nowhere! And another question is **when** did He do it? Never!

A careful look at the context of Chapter 13 reveals that Paul was teaching here that *without love* the Gifts were of no effect, and that they would never be perfectly used until **love** is the motive behind the Gifts. It goes on to say, in verse 11 and 12,

> *"When I was a child I spoke like a child, I understood as a child, I thought as a child; but when I became a man I put away childish things. For now we see through a glass darkly; but then face to face: now I know in part; but then shall I know even as I am known"*

It is so obvious to me that He is **speaking here of walking step by step to emotional maturity.** When you are childish, you only see in part. As you mature in Christ you are expected to walk in prophecy, receive a tongue, and walk in a more unselfish, mature love than a child would.

"That which is Perfect" has not come in that Jesus has not yet come back to Earth as a King. He has come first only as a Lamb. The weapons and the Gifts He gave us to use against the Enemy's forces will not pass away until He *comes again.* **He gave them to the church HIMSELF,** and when He returns as the reigning King, these things will no longer be needed because Satan will be bound in the Pit for 1,000 years, unable to fight us. See Revelation 20.

That passage also stated that knowledge would vanish away. **Knowledge has increased** so powerfully that it has been estimated that in the last 10 years, man has attained more knowledge than in the previous 6,000 years. Does that seem to support the fact that knowledge is vanishing?

Brothers and sisters in the Lord, as believers, you will be able to do these supernatural acts. These ministries are valid today. In fact, **you have a responsibility to carry out these ministries that God may receive the glory through you.**

The ministry of deliverance is not one that makes you or your church popular. You can expect much resistance if you get into this area because it is the one Satan fears most. He doesn't mind if you go to church as long as you **don't learn to put your faith into action against him.** You are no hinderance to keep him from harming your family, neighborhood or church if you **aren't using** your authority and words actively against Him.

If you want to learn more about demons, I would recommend the following books:

1. *Angels of Light* by Freeman Hobart (1993, Faith Ministries and Publications, Warsaw Publications)

2. *Pigs in the Parlor* by Hammond (Impact Books, Inc. 137 W. Jefferson Ave. Kirkwood, MO 63122)

3. *Demons and Eye-Witness Accounts* by Howard Pittman (Howard Pittman, Box 107, Foxworth MS, 39483)

4. *Clara Villaneuva* by Lester Sumrall (Lester Sumrall, 2315 S. Michigan St., South Bend, Indiana)

5. *Blumhardt's Battle* by Boshold (1970, Thomas Lowe Ltd., New York)
This lists dramatic accounts of deliverance in the eighteenth century by a man who was not familiar with what he was doing. The demons played games with him that are incredible. Do not read this book if you are easily emotionally disturbed, and do not let children read it.

6. *Surgeon of the Rusty Knife* by John Fuller (1974, Crowell, New York)

The story of a Brazilian Indian with supernatural ability to operate on people without anesthetic. A team of U.S. doctors investigated and verified the reports of his operations. I believe the man was possessed by a demon previously in a doctor in Germany. Note that it was not the spirit of the deceased doctor, but the demon, who possessed him while he was alive.

Two last words of caution.

1.) Demons work through doctrine. Scripture refers to *"doctrines of devils"* (I Timothy 4:1) and some churches actually advocate doctrines that came from devils. Beware of doctrines that teach the constant repetition of certain **acts**; repetitious prayer, communion served wrongly, etc. I have delivered people from demons that were **driving** people to say this prayer or do that action over and over to be saved. Jesus cautioned us about vain repetition, and this is the extreme of that warning. **Extreme doctrines** are a good key to devilish activity.

2.) Demons also work through **Christians who have had a backgrounds in psychic leadership** but have not yet repented and rejected their association with the occult, and gone through deliverance from those demons. Until they do, confusion will rule their ministry. I saw this take place many times. Here are two examples so you will know what to look for.

I attended a service where an evangelist was speaking. As I sat in the congregation my mind began to wander. I started daydreaming about how wonderful it would be if someday, after a heavy rain, I looked out the window of my house that overlooks an ordinarily dry creek-bed and saw nuggets of gold lying exposed just waiting to be picked up. As I was thinking this, the evangelist stopped teaching and came down the aisle to me. He said, "Brother, I see gold in your life. I see gold in your life! I don't know what this means, but I see gold in your life." He was not operating in the Spirit, but was reading my mind as he had been able to do in his psychic abilities from the occult.

On another occasion, a member of my family, who had previously had a tubal ligation to prevent pregnancy, was desiring to have a child. She had wished and wished for a miracle of restoration of her tubes so that she could have a child. Doctors have confirmed that when a woman so intensely desires a child, she can develop symptoms of pregnancy. A young evangelist came to our church during that time and supposedly, through a Word of Knowledge, said to her, "I see that you are pregnant and going to have a child." He had known nothing about her desires. She was later checked by a doctor and told that she definitely was not pregnant. I called the young man and talked with him about this. He admitted to having had psychic experiences prior to his salvation, and he was reading her mind. The "word of knowledge" he gave her was actually demonic influence! He had read her mind and saw what she was imagining. He needed to be delivered of a psychic spirit.

I give you the above examples to make you aware that while these supernatural occurrences are for The Church today, they need to be in operation **only under the power of the Holy Spirit.** We must constantly ask the Holy Spirit for the ability to discern the difference between the real and the imitations by the enemy. The more the world becomes ensnared by the devil's last attempts to seduce people as his end draws short, the more we need these Gifts to take the world for Christ.

As you depend on God and become familiar with Him and His character, you will be able to confidently step out into the ministry of deliverance with His authority and the operation

of the Gifts of the Spirit.

Be sure to read the following chapter on "Curses." They are in a class by themselves.

Chapter Ten
Curses, Witchcraft and Satanic Subtlety

Because this book is written to be informative in as many aspects as possible, I have added this short chapter to cover a very important area of spiritual warfare. We could sub-title this Chapter **"Unexplained Problems,"** which at times defy reason, especially for those, who, to the best of their understanding, are living a committed Christian life.

I have personally experienced the effects of curses placed against me, and had to rely on the Holy Spirit to teach me what was happening to me. Since I had been involved in deliverance ministry for so many years, the Satanic world was constantly looking for people whom they could use to curse me. God showed me there were many assignments against me.

I experienced times of **unexplained** depression, that had no reason to exist. I would **suddenly** become emotionally or physically exhausted, when just prior to the exhaustion I had felt fine. This was so unusual that I questioned God. I share with you what He showed me.

Many times this unexplained condition indicates that someone has spoken a curse against you.

In the middle of my own quest for revelation on the matter of curses, I was personally blessed to find, the book *CURSES; What They Are And How To Break Them* by Dick Bernal (Companion Press). It confirmed what I was learning from the Spirit about how to break them. Since I did not know that any other book on the subject of curses even existed, this find was very timely! I highly recommend it.

God is so good to show us how we need one another when it comes to battling the enemy! **Sharing revelation with one another is part of the strengthening of the Church in spiritual warfare.** Soldiers must stand together. I continued my search with much of Dick Bernal's insight tucked under my belt!

Ephesians 6:11 says that the devil uses "wiles" (trickery, cunning, a seductive procedure) against us. Verse twelve then says that,

> *"we wrestle not against flesh and blood* (i.e., people) *"but against principalities* (spiritual authorities), *against powers, against the **rulers of darkness** of this world, against **spiritual wickedness** in high places"*

...or, in plainer words, we are fighting against everything the devil does.

Note the key phrase in this verse is **"we wrestle."** Whether you are conscious of this or not, it doesn't change the fact that the devil **is constantly fighting** against us, using his strategy against our weakest points. He *"goes about like a roaring lion, seeking someone to devour"* (I Peter 5:8). We must always be watching and ready to fight, armed with the Word of God for protection.

No one is immune from his attacks, and so we must never forget that battle strategy of Ephesians 6:13-18 where God tells us to dress for that battle with the **right** armor, which are His words. **We must have at our immediate disposal fresh Words from God gotten in daily devotions with Him in His Word.**

In the area of curses, we can't know which **current battle strategy** is being used against us and how to use which armor, unless **the Holy Spirit reveals it to us!** He can tell you what curses are being spoken against you and how you can reverse them, **turning them around and back to the sender.**

How many times do we anger someone, maybe unintentionally, who then **speaks a curse out loud (invocation) against us**? Verbal utterances are extremely powerful. We all too often say it is important to "watch what you say," and then say negative or hurtful things anyway.

These can even come from Christians, as well as unbelievers, who do not know the **power** of their spoken thoughts against others, and the seriousness of their loose words. Words like "I hope you never can do that again," "I hope you never have money," "I hope your car breaks down," or "I hope you never teach again," are not idle words. They carry power and the **power** of words can bring **either** blessings **or** curses.

*"Therewith we both **bless** God and **curse** men. Out of the same mouth proceedeth blessing and cursing. My brethren these things ought not to be so."*
James 3:10

"The tongue is a fire, a world of iniquity ... and sets on fire the course of nature, and it is set on fire of hell."
James 3:6

Devilish power uses someone's tongue to make it "hell on earth" for you, until you learn to recognize it, and **remove the curse** with the same **spiritual authority** that Jesus had and gave us to use.

I know of a committed Christian lady who suffered unbelievably for nine years with unexplained physical pain and emotional stress. Feeling that she had been thrust away from the Lord violently, she was unable to make any sense of spiritual truths any more. This increased and became excruciatingly painful for about four of those nine years. Her mind was totally blank, and she felt like she was dangling over hell by an invisible thread, connected to nothing, empty and abandoned. She loved God down deep in her heart, but wanted nothing to do with any church, any people, or anything that had to do with the Lord.

From this you can understand that **curses are hidden** but can destroy a person. Without **spiritual gifts of discernment** in the Church these things will not ever be revealed. People will just go on suffering, thinking there is no cure and they just have to endure miserable lives. This is not something to play with or take lightly. It happens to believers so much more often than we want to think. This is not the work of devils. It is the work of the flesh against each other.

The Bible mentions curses over 125 times. These curses are serious and have not been taught fully by the Church. **But unexplained physical, emotional and spiritual problems that do not have any explanations are often the result of a curse of this type.**

Note that we are not talking here about generational curses (spoken about later), or about the general "curse of the law" spoken of in Galatians 3, but **about those individual curses that are personally spoken against us by name,** either by jealous Christians, people whom we may have angered, or those who, for whatever reason, want us hurt or our ministry ruined.

Now, the length of time it takes you to become aware of the problem and break it, is usually the same length of time it takes your body to recover the effects of it, **so seeing it quickly by His Holy Spirit** is imperative.

As soon as you are aware of what it is, you need to:

1.) speak out loud to the curse,

2.) command that it leave, and that it may not stay

around,

3.) and command that it return to its Sender.

Your recovery will start at once.

A good Scripture to constantly use against this kind of curse from then on is found in Isaiah 54:17,

"No curse formed against me shall prosper; and every tongue that shall rise against me in judgment thou shalt condemn. This is the heritage of the servants of the Lord!"

A common problem, spoken of earlier regarding generational curses, revolves around **the ones that have been passed down to us from our own forefathers.** We have little understanding about what our great-grandparents were spiritually involved with, and what has come upon us because of some form of evil they might have practiced, even innocently.

*"The sins of the father are upon the children to **the third and fourth** generations... "*

Exodus 20:5

I can remember when it was quite popular many years ago to have your tea leaves read or go to a fortune teller for entertainment. Reading and believing horoscopes (a ridiculous guide since every paper had different guidance) are also open doors to the enemy's harassment because **seeking direction from any source besides God's Word** is an open invitation for curses to come.

Perhaps we did not know that our ancestors did these things. It still affects us to our third and fourth generations— **until you can use your tongue to proclaim** that the curse is broken and that the blessings of Abraham are ours in Christ (Galatians 3:14). So, although the sins of the fathers extend down through three generations, it also says in the same verse in Exodus, that believers, *"who love Him and keep His commandments"* can have mercy for the same time period,

> *"...and showing mercy unto thousands of them that love me and keep My commandments."*
>
> Exodus 20:6

Now, **do it out loud,** claiming the Word of God, something like this;

> **"Although the sins of my fathers have come to me and my children, down to the third and fourth generation, God now shows mercy to me and thousands of my heirs because I love Him and keep His commandments. Therefore, I break all curses** (of poverty, anger, jealousy, fear, whatever it is) **formed against us!"**

If you gave your life to the Lord and now love Him and keep His commandments, your children can now live under that blessing as you cancel out the old curse.

Speak to the problem and to the devils bringing the harassment, renouncing all occult activities that your ancestors may have been in, repenting of it **for** them, and confessing their sins. This was a common confession in the Old Testament. Even the dear prophets asked God to forgive the sins of the people that were sinning against God, though the prophets themselves were not sinning. **This may have to be done quite a few times until the cursers and their messengers get the idea and remain gone.** Keep up the good fight until it's won!

Constant repetitions of the same **unusual or unexplained happenings** are clues to old family curses still held against you.

One family I knew constantly had bones broken. When we broke the curse out loud it stopped. Another family was always fearing that poverty was going to overtake them as it had for generations. Once these curses were commanded out loud to stop their operation, finances began to come in to meet their needs.

Witchcraft takes many forms, some of which seem too innocent to be concerned with. This is deceiving. For example, the prayer of a concerned Christian, worried about another brother's salvation, may pray like this. "God, make them get saved, **no matter what it takes,** to bring them to their knees."

When we use this type of "prayer," we are attempting to force our will (control) over them.[5] The wrong spirit can use this to create severe problems. A devil can take this prayer that is not of God and use "no matter what" to the person's destruction. **This is so close to intentional witchcraft as to be put into the same category. We need to bless, and not curse, with our prayers.**

Witchcraft and the occult go together since the same demonic power is behind both. Witches send **intentional curses,** or work through incantations against people. Psychics, New Age Teaching (although this is not really "new," but just a resurrected variation of many old teachings), charms, "god's eyes," Kachina dolls, etc., are all items of the occult and need to be gotten rid of, **even though they seem unintentional.** Go through your house and check for anything that has

---

[5] Instead, pray something like "Lord, I release them to the revelation knowledge of Jesus."

connections to these things.[6] Remove them. **Whatever they cost you is not worth the harm they can draw to you. You will be** surprised how much better your home will feel.

We must keep up the fight to have authority over the enemy in ALL areas, **preparing the Earth for the Lord's return.** Satanic subtlety should be exposed by His people every single day until it's done, and He can say, "Well done, you good and faithful servant!"

The restoration of the Church to its full perfection is going to include doing the priestly duties. Remembering I Peter, *"We are priests to God and to each other."* Part of the priestly duties was to bless people, which is the direct opposite power of cursing.

God is a blesser and we should be also. Jesus said,

"Bless those who curse you and do good to those that despitefully use you."

Luke 6:27

So, although we send the curse back, we also bless the person who sent it and forgive them, leaving vengeance only to God. We do not use returning a curse as a tool to curse others. Romans 12:14 says,

"Bless them which persecute you; and curse not.

---

[6] Some additional items to look for are likenesses of Satan or demons and ouija boards. Also search for items connected with or **books about:** table tipping, spiritualism, black arts, tarot cards, levitation, clairvoyance, scientology, numerology, tea-leaf reading, phrenology, colorology, automatic writing, pendulum healing, psychic portraits, crystals, rosicrucianism, yoga, pentagrams, astral projection, fortune telling, talismans, astrology and voo-doo dolls.

Not rendering evil for evil, or railing for railing but contrariwise blessing knowing that ye are thereunto called that ye should inherit a blessing. For he that will love life, and see good days, let him refrain his tongue from evil and his lips that they speak not guile."

I Peter 3:9,10

You can see from this chapter that we have dealt with 4 kinds of curses.

1.) the curse of the Law

2.) generational curses

3.) railings

4.) personal curses spoken against

When we return a personal curse against us, we are **not cursing** the sender. We are just **returning the curse** to them that they may learn not to do it anymore. How many innocent people have they cursed that need set free, if only they could identify them? The original senders must be stopped for the good of the many, and we have the authority to do it.

These are serious matters, and the present Church as a whole is learning more and more about this as we get closer to the end of world, **facing more rampant wickedness, even** *in the apostate church*, than we have ever seen before!

The stronger voices of **the Prophet who must warn**, and **the Apostle who upholds true doctrine** are going to be heard more and more even though the lukewarm Laodicean Church we live in says, "Oh, please don't say such unloving words to us!"

This discipline must be heard and obeyed if the TRUE

Church is to be perfected into the righteous, purified bride of Revelation 21 and 22.

Are you willing?

Chapter Eleven
Healing

In the first edition of this book, I put this Healing Chapter earlier. However, **healing is such an important sister to deliverance** that I am placing it here.

When a person has had demons, the nesting place of that demonic life has resulted in wounds to that part of the body. **Quite often it needs healing after the demons have left.**

So let's look at healing in general, and then later we will see how it applies to the delivered as well.

"Is there any sick among you? Let him pray. Is any merry? Let him sing psalms. Is any sick among you? Let him call for the elders of the church; and let them pray over him, anointing him with oil in the name of the Lord and the prayer of faith shall save the sick, and the Lord shall raise him up, and if he have committed sins, they shall be forgiven him."

James 5:13

We are told to call for the elders (those who are recognized as spiritually mature in the Word) of the church. We aren't told to call for the doctor or the druggist or even the dentist. **We are told** to call the elders of the church who are to pray.

It is so important for the sick person "to call for" (summon) the elders, because that brings the sick person and the one who is to pray into agreement (Matthew 18:19). **If someone else calls for prayer other than the one who is ill, the one praying often wonders if the sick person really wants to be**

158

healed. (That may sound strange, but I have known many people who didn't want to let loose of their illness because they wanted to be dependent on the ones who served them.) That hinders agreement in faith which is so conducive to receiving healing. Of course there are times when the sick person can NOT do that, and then the prayer of the friend can be substituted, but it isn't as strong as a prayer of agreement most of the time.

Again and again I've heard people say, "I didn't come to church because I was ill." **Well, that's the precise time you need to be IN church if at all possible!**

What better place to pray for the sick than in the church service where His promise is that He will come where two or more are gathered in His Name? (Matthew 18:20) Notice that this scripture comes directly after the Scripture about agreement quoted above. Agreement and His presence make a powerful combination, a charged atmosphere in which to receive His goodness!

Being where believers are, and not in a hospital room where there is often unbelief in family members (because of their fears and emotional attachments), or hospital staff (because of their dependence on medicine only) **is very important; so much so that even Jesus had to remove unbelievers before he raised the daughter of the leader of the synagogue (Luke 8:51).**

Faith does not add, as we learned earlier, but unbelief and doubt are huge deterrents, so remove them, if necessary, before healing. Sometimes, my faith was so high that curious unbelievers didn't keep a healing from coming, and Jesus did this often. *So healing can happen* when your faith is great, even when doubters are present. Keep you faith renewed in the Word, getting stronger and stronger, and you will get better and better at it.

Healing, whether in the natural or the spiritual, is a process.[7] It takes time to accomplish. When you pray for a person to be healed, the same process takes place supernaturally that would take place if the person swallowed the proper medication to produce healing.

The medication would first go to the stomach, be digested, pass through the blood stream, then go to the area of the problem and take care of it. The healing is happening.

It is the same with prayer. When you have prayed for someone who is ill, let them know that the work has already been done, just as if they had taken a one-time medication. The healing is happening in unseen places as God is rearranging the molecules, enzymes and chemicals in the system. If they could see it in a microscope they would believe the manifestation. **Just because it hasn't built up to be big enough to see with the naked eye** *does not mean it isn't physically taking place!*

The person may not **feel like** he or she is healed after being prayed for, but if they had swallowed medication, they wouldn't **feel like** they had been healed yet either. **Faith is believing that what God can see is happening physically even when you cannot see it yet.**

Healing has already been provided for by His stripes before the cross. We know this because Peter (who was the first disciple we know of to have faith to heal after Jesus went to Heaven) wrote, speaking of Jesus,

"Who His own self bare our sins in His own body on the tree, that we, being dead to sins, should live unto

---

[7] Instant healings can be classified as miracles.

righteousness; by whose stripes ye were healed."

I Peter 2:24

It has **already** been done. That word *"were"* is past tense, an accomplished fact. **Peter could heal because He believed this.** He had learned it from Jesus, The Living Word, and also believed the Prophecy of Isaiah, the Written Word, which said,

"But He was wounded for our transgressions, he was bruised for our iniquities; the chastisement of our peace was upon him; and with his stripes we are healed."

Isaiah 53:5

There it is again in the past tense. Peter's **faith in God's Word** opened up the channels for God to work through.

"Without faith it is impossible to please God."

Hebrews 11:6

This is what God is always after, our love and trust in His Living Word and His Written Word.

To expect to feel instant healing with prayer is to expect a miracle. In our I Corinthians list of gifts, **The Gift of Healing and the Gift of Miracles are both listed because they are different.** Realize, though, that a miracle is an instant happening: a healing is sure but gradual. The Gift of Miracles will be explained in more detail later.

Encourage the person you are praying for **not to doubt** that their healing is already accomplished according to God's Word. If they doubt, it's too hard for their bodies to receive what they asked for. Help them to visualize what is really happening to their body because of what the Word says.

Doubt is believing what you feel more than you believe what God says He has done. Doubt is a very strong deterrent.

Jesus cautioned His followers very strongly about doubt.

*"For verily I say unto you, That whosoever shall say unto this mountain, Be thou removed, and be thou cast into the sea, **and shall not doubt in his heart**, but shall believe that those things which he saith shall come to pass; he shall have whatsoever he saith."*

Mark 11:23

When we find ourselves doubting, we needn't feel condemned. Doubt is just human reaction (like fear or anger) which we can allow God to constantly work on, so we can be more like Him. God will finish in you the faith He authored when you gave your life to Him. He is the Author and finisher of your faith (Hebrews 12:2).

Don't ever let the enemy make you feel guilty for doubting. Only the enemy, never God, will lay a guilt-trip on you for doubting. God will only **remind you** not to doubt. Then, all you have to do is stop, quickly ask God to forgive you for doubting, and continue to work on building up your faith again in His Word. **His grace to forgive and keep on teaching us is always there.**

*"There is now therefore **no condemnation** to them which are in Christ Jesus..."*

Romans 8:1

The father of a child who was hurt constantly by demons asked Jesus for help. Jesus' answer to Him was,

"If you can believe, all things are possible to him that believes."

Mark 9:23

This man instantly knew he did not have that kind of faith and answered so truthfully,

"Lord, I believe; Help Thou my unbelief!"

Mark 9:24

Jesus honored this man's honesty and dependence on Him by healing his son. We can always be this truthful with God as we ask, seek and knock for more faith to believe. It is there and available for the Church.

Each church should make time for healing services even when healings don't occur in every case. That is no reason to do away with healing services. That's God's business, and He will show His people **by experience** what is needed in each individual case as we first obey Him and *do the word, not be hearers only* (James 1:22).

This is similar to faith and hope. Faith is instant. Hope is future.

Jesus gave the power to heal the Church. He was beaten for it. Jesus went through extreme pain and humiliation **before He was crucified** when He was beaten almost to death with thirty-nine lashings of a whip. It was common practice for a Roman prisoner to receive a scourging of "forty-minus-one stripes" which they believed was one blow less than what it took to kill a man (John 19:1, II Corinthians 11:24).

Those stripes did not apply to our spiritual salvation but to our healing. He did this to fulfill that Isaiah 53 prophecy where Isaiah **looked forward into the future** and saw that those stripes would provide our healing. Peter had **looked back on the scourging** and stated that those stripes He bore brought us healing (I Peter 2:24).

In Old Testament times, when the bull, sheep or goats were brought to the temple to be sacrificed for the peoples' sins, as God had taught them to, **they were never tied up and beaten first with a whip.** That practice would have been unacceptable. The sins of the people were laid on the sacrificial lamb first through the priest's hands. Then it was killed and offered up to God to cleanse the people from their sins.

The Old Testament types, or examples, are fulfilled in the New Testament. **Jesus was the New Testament offering.** John correctly called Him,

> *"the **Lamb** of God which taketh away the sins of the world."*
>
> John 1:29

Since the **Old Testament sacrificial lambs** were not beaten before they were offered for sins, then Jesus, **the New Testament sacrificial Lamb**, couldn't be beaten for our sins either.

Scripture teaches that

> *"without the **shedding of blood**, there is no remission for sins"*
>
> Hebrews 9:22

Shedding means voluntarily giving up your life's blood supply until death occurs. His whole life was what He gave for our sins. **He gave His life's blood for our sins, and endured the beating for our sicknesses!**

Jesus went **beyond** the sin question and allowed Himself to be scourged by taking the stripes first, before offering His whole self for sin. Why? He didn't have to go through scourging to free you from sin. His death would do that. He did it so you and I could have access to physical healing **as well as** the redeeming of our soul. **If forgiveness of our sins required the stripes of the scourging, the cross was not sufficient to save us from the results of our sinning.** It would have taken both Jesus' death on the cross and His beating to have forgiven your sins. And that was **not** in the Old Testament type, so it couldn't be so.

That proves that Jesus took our diseases for us, and not, as some churches teach, that everything he suffered was just for our salvation from sin.

NOW, HOW DO WE HEAL?

We look carefully at how Jesus healed and *do exactly the same thing;*

no matter what our favorite pastor has taught for twenty-five years,

no matter what our dear, saintly mothers have said,

no matter what we have heard from inspiring people,

no matter how long it takes us to learn from Him.

Jesus is the only sure way. Only He had one-hundred percent success!

He knew, even as He showed His disciples how to heal, that He was going to be beaten in order to release healing to the Earth. So the first step is to have that fact clearly settled in our minds as we watch Him heal in the Word.

Jesus went about all of Galilee teaching in the synagogues and preaching the Gospel, and "healing **all** manner of sickness and **all** manner of disease among the people" (Matthew 10:1 and many, many other places in Scripture). His fame spread throughout the region so much so that people came, and then brought to Him as many other people as they could get to Him, and when He spoke to the problem every single sickness and disease was healed. All of them. Hundreds of them! Probably thousands!

No one was told they would have to wait a few months "because the sickness is God's way of making you more patient, Dear." People only use this excuse when they are understandably frustrated that their hopes for healing have not come true yet. **But we can't let this change our clear strategy of letting Jesus' example continue to show us how healing is attained!**

Neither can you say truthfully that, as some teach, "You are sick for the Glory of God." That is a lie. **He gets glory when you are healed!**

Jesus has not somehow changed His intention or motives. His heart went out to them because He had so much compassion that He healed them. He is just the same today as He ever was. Paul knew this when He said, *"Jesus, the same yesterday, today and forever"* (Hebrews 13:8). **If healings were commonplace during the New Testament Era, and they aren't commonplace today, someone changed! It was the Church, *not Jesus!***

When other believers and I first started to ask God to use us in healing **because we saw it in Jesus and knew it had to be in the Church,** we had all the fears and doubts that you do. But we just had to be His Bride and could not disappoint Him, and so we risked our reputations and fears of failure and just started laying hands on people and speaking the same Words Jesus did. "Be healed." "Be whole."

And slowly, but surely, we saw His faithfulness to His own words as we got better and better at it. Every healing gave us more faith for the next opportunity. Every failure was discouraging, but we just kept reading the Word and determining to believe it and try again, and again, and again.

Headaches were healed. Chronic bad backs were healed. Arthritis was healed. Bad hearts were healed. Teeth were filled with gold. Cancer was healed. **We were amazed as on and on it went. We only knew a little but we acted on what we knew. That's the real key.**

A wonderful way to increase your faith to believe for healings is to look up every place where Jesus healed and see what He **said** to each person. You will notice He NEVER said "God, heal this person." He NEVER asked God to heal: He commanded healing to happen. He said things like, "Be healed" or "Lazarus, arise", or "Be thou clean." We ask God (pray) for what to say and then speak to the body of the person, **as Jesus did**.

On one of my trips to Nigeria, in a mud-thatched church, a sixteen-year-old boy who had never spoken a word in his life was brought to me. **I laid hands on him and spoke healing to him. I saw no manifestation of healing.** He went back to his seat, and I worked with some other people, and after a while the service was over. I thought no more about him until, as we were leaving town, a young man came to say goodbye to me in a large group of well-wishers. My interpreter told me that that young man was the same one who had been silent all his life! **He had been so totally healed** that he didn't even have to learn the language as a child does when he begins to learn to speak as a baby.

I asked why no one had told me he had been healed, and they said they thought I automatically knew when healing took place. You will not know most of the time, **so you must believe that what you have commanded to be is so**, and do not just believe what you see! You have **agreed with God** that healing in Jesus' Name works, so it does.

This agreement is a powerful healing strategy. Remember when Jesus said,

> *"Verily I say unto you, 'Whatsoever ye shall bind on earth shall be bound in heaven'"* (i.e., if you bind sickness on Earth, I'll **agree** with you from heaven), *And whatsoever ye shall loose on earth shall be loosed in heaven...* (i.e., if you loose healing on Earth, I'll **agree** with you from heaven)"
>
> Matthew 18:18

Then, immediately following, He emphasized this principle even further by saying,

> *"Again, I say unto you, that if two of you shall **agree** on **Earth** as touching ANYTHING that they shall ask, it shall be done for them of my **Father** which is in heaven."*
>
> Matthew 18:19

For years I thought the Church knew what these Scriptures meant, but now I see that **agreement with God** (that's two), and agreement with Him **and each other** (that's three, or more) **constitute a strength that the enemy has to bow to.** Every time a healing happened it was because Jesus and the Father were **agreeing.** Jesus said,

> *"Whatsoever I speak therefore even as the Father said unto me, so I speak."*
>
> John 12:50

Verbal agreement. There it is again. Whether the problem is disunity in the church, disunity in the body (illness), disunity in the mind (anything from mild confusion to insanity), the agreement with God and/or each other can reverse chaos into order.

Healing is the perfect orderly arrangement of the body that

God originally intended for Mankind before sin entered and confused His world. Verbally agree that whatever the problem, it is being dealt with, and it will go away like it did when Jesus and the Father agreed.

Did you ever notice that when Jesus raised Lazarus from the dead, that in front of the people He verbally **agreed with the Father** that since They had **already agreed,** it was going to be done? Listen.

> *"Father, I thank Thee that Thou hast heard me. And I knew that thou hearest me always; but **because of the people which stand by me I said it,** that they may believe that Thou hast sent Me."*
>
> John 11:42

He and His Father had already agreed. Now He wanted the people to see that so that they would know and agree too.

Jesus' words about agreement show just how much authority the Church really possesses. This is not a prayer, and requires no great faith. There couldn't be anything easier! Do it, Church. Do it! Only in DOING it will you get better and better at it.

Jesus' parable of the talents in Matthew 25:14-30 was about being **faithful in using the little amounts that we have, so that He can THEN trust us with more.** Speak healing to those who are sick now, today, and God will give you more as you need it later.

> *"Thou has been faithful over a few things, I will therefore make thee ruler over many things."*
>
> Matthew 25:23

Peter did it. He first healed the lame man in front of the temple (the story I narrated in Chapter 1). The man had been crippled all His life, but he leaped up, walked around, and entered the temple praising God. The book of Acts tells of believers bringing the sick so that even if Peter's shadow fell on them, they were healed. Those with unclean spirits were healed. **Peter was agreeing with the words and examples that Jesus had given him. We must do the same.**

Paul and Barnabus, not part of the original twelve Apostles, also healed the sick. They preached the Words that Jesus taught them, and signs and wonders followed them. You can agree with Jesus and them and do the same. **The power was given to the Church, not just the Twelve.**

Philip was another example. He was one of the first deacons, and it was his job to wait on tables and feed the widows and the children. He had no spiritual appointment or title in the church of Jerusalem, but God had a job for him. Philip went to Samaria and preached Christ to the people there. All the people listened to him and saw the miracles he did (Acts 8:6). Unclean spirits crying in loud voices came out of many, and many lame were healed. There was rejoicing in that city because of Philip's willingness to agree with God and be used by Him to set the people free. **Read it all in Acts 8, and be lifted in your spirit to do the works of God!**

In the Old Testament, Moses and Aaron and Samson and the Judges and Samuel and Elijah and Elisha and Isaiah worked miracles. **All of them were different.** Some were weak and some were strong, but **they agreed with God so He could use them!**

In the New Testament there were many more than those just mentioned. There were the seventy, and there was Stephen. **There was a constant flow of miracles worked by various men because miracles are a part of the character of God.** God is still writing His will and testament through you and me. Do you want to be part of it?

Because I **expect to see miracles** accomplished today I am seeing them. Because I **just agree with God** that His words are so concerning Himself I see miracles. Because I agree with God about me, one of the least of His Church, I see miracles. I know of a few who are doing the same around the world. But if Jesus is to come, there must be more. There must be people willing to be made into His perfected Bride, ready to rule and reign over the **Universe** with Him, **as soon as we have learned how to do it on this little planet.**

One last thing that we have found; **miracles often take place during a time of praise and worship.** In turn, miracles lead to more praise and worship being offered to God. When Jesus rode into Jerusalem, the throngs praised and worshipped Him. The Pharisees condemned the noise as being improper. Jesus, however, said that if the people hadn't praised Him, the rocks and stones would have!

King David, a man after God's own heart, gave beautiful examples of **praising the Lord with a loud voice, praising Him with uplifted hands, and with many instruments.** Are you anxious to see healings and miracles in your church services? Then read David's Psalms and ask the Lord to show you through them the true meaning of praise and worship.

David said in Psalms 149 and 150 that the people were to let the praises of God be in their "MOUTHS" (i.e., out loud), and to

> "sing unto the Lord a new song (i.e., fresh, not boring)
> praise Him in the congregation of the saints,
> praise Him in the firmament of His power,
> praise Him for His might acts,
> praise Him according to His excellent greatness,
> praise Him with the sound of the trumpet,
> praise Him with the psalstery and harp,
> praise Him with the timbrel and the dance,
> praise Him with the stringed instruments and organs,

praise Him on the loud cymbals,
praise Him with the high-sounding cymbals,
LET EVERYTHING THAT HATH BREATH
PRAISE THE LORD!"

Do you think He really means praise is important?! Do you think that doing things "decently and in order" means that we should sing our hymns without emotion? or without excitement? or quietly to ourselves? ... certainly not according to the sound of those instruments He names! **We have great reasons to be excited and let God know how He makes us feel about His greatness!** He tells us to because He loves it! Prayer, which is so important, is **talking** with God. But Praise is **giving** to God. It blesses Him.

This is the way the early church operated. This is the way the present-day Church should operate. A pathologist friend of mine says that all physicians agree that the body is designed **to heal itself,** and that medicines only help that system to kick-in better when something has gone wrong.

Imagine! God designed your body to be well, not sick. So if it gets sick He is willing to heal it **if you will just agree with Him, and believe it is so.**

Chapter 12
How to Get From Here To There

Although mankind almost destroyed the true Church during the Dark Ages, **it is gradually being brought back by believers who are taking a good, more honest and intense look at the Word again!** God is compelling them and they are listening!

They are truly beginning to see that Jesus is ready to return as soon as **His Church chooses to let Him make her ready!** They want whatever it takes to be restored and follow the example Jesus gave them, going about tending to the works of God.

"And behold there came a leper and worshipped Him saying, 'Lord, if You will You can make me clean.' And Jesus put forth His hand and touched him, saying, 'I will; be thou clean.' And immediately his leprosy was cleaned."

Matthew 8:3

Jesus was so moved by compassion that He was compelled by love to heal the sick. When He saw the multitudes following Him hungering for his teachings, He was moved with compassion. He saw them as sheep without a shepherd. **He indicated that one of the identifying marks of His Church would be compassion.** I believe that if the Church cared enough about people in trouble it would have a compelling desire to help.

I first got into this walk in my thirties and was attending a Full-Gospel denominational church that taught about salvation, healings and the Gifts, **but no one was getting healed or delivered and new converts were very rare.** When I wanted more of what I saw in the Word I was reprimanded by the pastor and elders for hungering for more than I should have. But I knew the Bible *had to be true*, so I kept studying, telling other interested believers what I was getting from the Lord, and pretty soon the healing started happening and people were getting saved.

This was very scary because I was a rather shy and unsociable person. I would rather stay inside my house than go out into my own backyard if my neighbor was already in his and might require me to converse with him. But I loved to talk about the Word with "safe" people at church and in Bible Studies. When I saw that people were gathering around me, I told God, **"Oh please don't make me a pastor, you know I'm not the type."** But who else was going to get the hurting people free? That's where He got me!

He wanted His people free! He was compassionate and put His compassion for hurting people onto me. I became a pastor and learned, with others, how to heal and deliver. A young dear Nigerian pastor in Africa wrote me and asked me to come help him with his little struggling church, and without any denominational help my church sent me to him. Three times! Now he has fifty-seven churches!

I didn't know, any more than you do, how God was going to do this. I only started with just enough faith to start, and God was faithful as I took every next step. **He will do this for any person who wants to be His true Church more than anything else in the world.**

You will hear of people so moved with compassion that they perform heroic acts, jeopardizing their own lives to save others. Mothers run into burning buildings to get their children. Men jump into icy waters to rescue drowning people.

There are those we all have read of and admire who have sacrificed their will entirely and are doing nothing but meeting the needs of humanity. This is what Jesus meant when He said **we must lay down our lives for our brothers.** Have we lost that compassion that Jesus showed us?

Church, are you willing to give up the comfortable place you are in and risk losing it all in the sight of others so Jesus can use you in the Gift of Healing and Gift of Miracles? It's not for those who accidentally get it. **It's there for those who determine, because of inner compassion for hurting people, to go after it with all their might.**

Do you think that God sent those people you see and feel sorry for into **your** line of sight for **YOU** to heal? Why not? Who else will do it if you know the way to heal them, but **YOU** will not? This is why I originally entitled this book, *"Where Has My Church Gone?"* Ask God, "Am I really Your Church?"

A few of the people who read the first edition said, once they had gotten to this point, **"But tell me HOW to do it!"**

I have already!! I have treated you as Jesus treated His disciples in that:

* I have told you examples of how I have healed and delivered.

* I have told you why it works in the Spirit.

* I told you that only practice and experience will get you better at it.

If you are not yet doing it, is it because you haven't taken what you know and **gone** with it. He who is faithful to give away the little he has will be given more.

I have found no person yet who has given his life totally to this purpose that has not succeeded. Only those who say, "I cannot yet" or "I tried and it didn't work" have failed.

In Luke 9:1-2 Jesus sent His disciples out to minister without Him. He told them to 1.) have authority over all devils, 2.) cure diseases (fatal illnesses), 3.) preach the good news, and 4.) heal the sick (temporary illnesses). **Can you imagine how He expected them to do that after only two years of learning from Him?**

Any good theology teacher would have said they hadn't enough training yet! But Jesus knew they would learn more from experience than anything. And He made it even harder than we would ever make it on ourselves. He said to take no extra money, clothes or provisions. **He wanted them totally dependent on the Spirit, not on things or circumstances.** This is what we must do. Go try it.

The ministry of signs, wonders and miracles is valid and yours for today. God **still** imparts supernatural gifts to men.

We are not just sinners saved by grace. **We are co-equal heirs with Jesus** (Romans 8:17) and are empowered by the Holy Spirit, just as He was, to do what He said we could do.

God **does** have the answers to man's problems. He **does** have the cure. He **does** have the deliverance for spirit-produced illnesses. He **does** desire that you be in good health and prosper (III John 2). He **does** desire that you be able to go to Him for the answers to the difficult problems you face, just as a good earthly father who loves his child would welcome the opportunity to help that child. He **does** care for you.

Now how do we get from where we are to where we should be, occupied with doing the works of God? I am speaking to the Church, the saved body of Christ. If you are not born again, that becomes your starting point. Please see the Appendix at the end of this Chapter that I have prepared for you.

After salvation, **THE FIRST STEP** is to get intimate with the Bible. The Bible was written by God-selected men who were moved by the Holy Spirit. In other words, the Holy Spirit is the author of the Bible. When you have the Holy Spirit residing within you, you have the author of the Bible within you! **The Bible then becomes an open book to you as you study it.** Passages that were once difficult to understand will become quite clear. It is not a book of stories and fables. It is not incorrectly translated and most people who say it is have not spent years searching and studying it as God says we need to.

God **does have** the answers to man's problems. The trouble is that our **minds** tells us differently! Our world-programed-brains are always fighting against our Spirit-programed, born-again spirits.

So our minds need **washing!** They need to agree with what God is saying in our perfect, born-again spirits.

Brain-washing has been used for generations by evil men to make people believe lies. This is just another way the devil has tried to copy God's methods. The truth is, we need God's washing of our brains because it has been so garbaged up with the world's "answers" to our problems **instead of** God's answers.

"Husbands, love your wives, even as Christ also loved the Church and gave Himself for it, that He might sanctify and cleanse it with the washing of water BY THE WORD."
Ephesians 5:26

Only the Bible can wash out the old wrong reasonings and replace them with the Truth.

That brings me to **THE SECOND STEP** of growth, and that is to be filled with the SPIRIT.

Paul said we were to **"be filled" with the Spirit** (Ephesians 5:18). As explained in Chapter Five, this infilling of the Holy Spirit is not just an option. It is a command. The infilling of the Holy Spirit will enable you to become the vessel that is used of God to perform those signs, wonders and miracles. You will realize your potential, and will be an otherwise common ordinary man or woman who becomes uncommon and extraordinary in the service of God.

THE THIRD STEP is to be sure to incorporate praise and worship into your daily living. Go about singing psalms and praising God as you take care of everyday tasks. Once you get into a church service, you will then be ready to praise God because you will have already stirred up the Spirit within you before you got there (II Timothy 2:6). The Word says that God inhabits the praises of His people (Psalm 22:3). God actually dwells in the atmosphere of praise and worship. Think of that! When you praise God, God is attending to your praises and is there to heal, restore and deliver.

THE FOURTH STEP on the path from here to there is to be prepared to see a restoration between your church and the church down the street. All who claim Christ as their Savior and God as their Father are on the side of the battle against the enemy. This is regardless of what denominational name they may use and regardless of where they worship.

It is in the spirit of unity that the body of Christ can accomplish the most. I am **not** talking about a one-world church. But I am talking about extending love to your spiritual brothers and sisters who have been saved by Jesus' blood and have gifts that you don't have. We all need one another's Gifts of the Spirit.

Divisions over doctrinal differences **must thrill the heart of Satan who loves to see us separated.** Even he knows that there is great strength when many people are in agreement. When we get the proper attitude going toward our brothers and sisters, Satan had better watch out! He won't have a chance.

Recognize that our church buildings are a type of **"sheepshed"** where we come to be healed, delivered, strengthened, fed and watched over as needed. As we are strengthened by His Spirit and **one another,** we then go out and lead others to Jesus, bringing them into the Church for their feeding and care. They then go out and bring others in. A **continuous** growth.

There should be more salvations taking place outside the church than inside. It is not the Pastor's job to get people saved. It is his job to care for the sheep. Does a shepherd birth baby sheep? No. Sheep birth sheep! Sometimes sheep are born in the shed, but mostly they are born in the field.

This would be a simple undertaking **if we were operating in the fullness of the Spirit every weekday and then bringing what we know to the sheepshed.**

Then we could give what He had taught us to the other sheep as we allow Him to empower us during a service to walk in the Gifts with the evidences of signs, wonders and miracles following us.

Then we would have people following us to meet our God!

This restoration of the Church WILL come. **You** can be a part of it **IF** you make yourself available.

To be a part of it means being a part of the very last days' ministry of the Holy Spirit.

These are exciting times that are approaching! Those who recognize who they are through Jesus and how much authority they really have in Him **will be those on the cutting edge of the Church.** The battle is real. The authority is powerful and awesome!

Rise up, Church, and take your rightful place. Exercise your authority to bring defeat to Satan and usher in the second coming of our Lord.

Even so, Lord Jesus, come quickly!

Appendix

As I explained in an earlier Chapter, you must know Jesus as your Savior in order to be filled with the Holy Spirit. It was Jesus' sacrifice that enabled you to be filled with the Spirit and walk in power. If you wish to be saved from the kingdom of darkness where you are trapped if you are not saved, please pray this prayer.

Father, I know that I am a sinner. I repent of the things I have done that were done in my will and not in Yours. I know now that Jesus died for me and I accept His sacrificial death as payment for my sins.

Jesus, thank you for dying for me. I want you to be the Lord of my life from this day forward.

Holy Spirit, fill me with your presence and your power. Help me to be about the business of doing the works of God every day for the rest of my life. I love you, God, and will serve you with my whole life. Thank you for saving me.

I ask this in Jesus' name,

Amen!